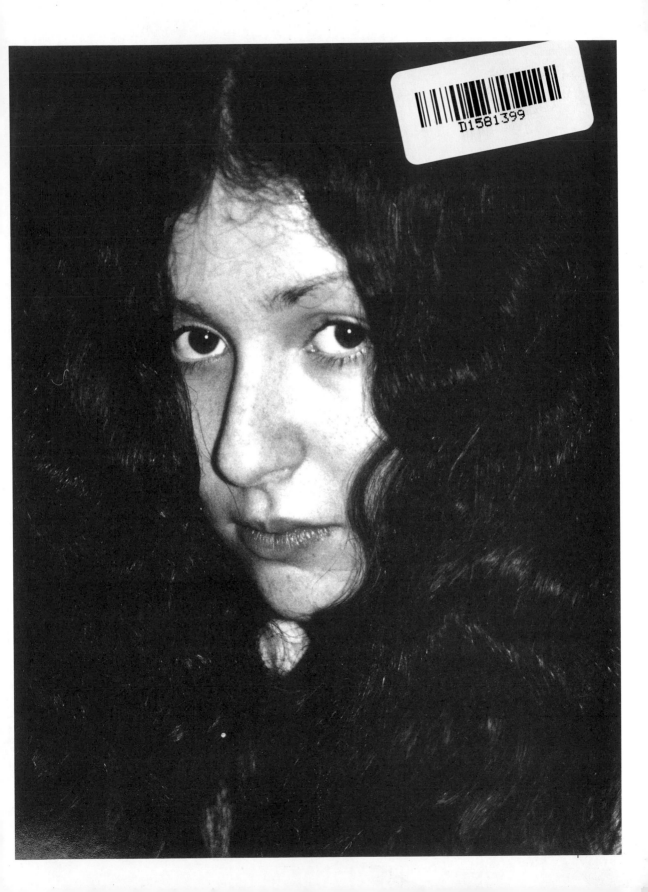

Standing Down Falling Up

Asperger's Syndrome from the Inside

by

Nita Jackson

Acknowledgments

I've got a huge tub of 'Miniature Heroes' which I will lovingly bestow upon the following people:

My mother, for devoting herself to the Asperger cause despite never being paid for it.
My family, for trying to tolerate me.
David Moat, for diagnosing me.
The Maudsley Group (Pam Yates & Co.), for offering their support.
Anne Pemberton, for her contribution on Irlen's syndrome.
William Marriage, for offering help.
The Social Skills Pilot Group (Gail Fisher & Co.) for setting up a
much-needed group on behalf of Asperger teenagers.
The *Asperger United* journal, for publicising my work.
Moyna Adams, for helping me back into education.
My teachers - Peter Osbourne, Mr. Doughty (first name unknown), Trish Taylor, Faith Moody,
Joel Tahoulin, Lesley Thomas, Faith Resmayer, Kevin Murphy, Sue Hathaway, Frank Jackson (& co) -
for putting up with me.

Michelle and Mike Connel for providing support, trust and encouragement.
Haley, for permitting me to use her letters in my book.
Andy Horesman and the Strathclyde Autistic Society, for allowing me to interview them.
Jo Douglas and NAS Northern Ireland, for also putting up with me.
Janet MacDonald for guiding me to a healthier lifestyle.
Anthony Lipski, Penny Deakin and everyone at Prospects, for helping me improve my work skills.
Sheela and the Barney Brothers (ha ha) from the BBC, for giving me my 15 minutes of regional fame.
Donna Williams, Clare Sainsbury and Liane Holiday Willey, for just being all-round excellent authors.
Karen Fisher & Co. at the Brentwood Theatre for providing excellent work experience!
The HENS, for agreeing to perform my play.

Jay, Kev, Stuart, Andy M, Jo, Peter, Emma A, Alex, Ollie, Kathy, Harry, Sam,
Paul S, Paul B, Joe, Andrew M and Andrew E.

Dedication
to Michelle Connel

Contents

Being in a minority, even a minority of one, did not make you mad. There was truth and there was untruth, and if you clung to the truth, even against the whole world, you were not mad.

(George Orwell *1984*, Penguin books, 1989)

We know the truth. The truth is Asperger's syndrome, not lunacy.
We know we're not mad.

Intro

Apart from the publisher's intervention, I'm a complete stranger to you, so allow me to introduce myself:

Hello there people, je suis Nita - the mad bird with Asperger's syndrome who wrote this book for anyone who is interested in 'getting inside the head' of an Asperger person - I hope you enjoy reading this account as much as I enjoyed writing it.

As you've probably guessed, I'm nowhere near sane! In fact, I'm regarded as a 'freak' by most people. Firstly because I like wearing luminous clothing in the day time, use goggles as a hair accessory, and often spray my hair bright yellow, pink or blue; secondly because basically I'm just B-ZAR!! I'm an eccentric as well as an 'Aspee'; thirdly, because I squeeze into clothes two sizes too small for me (I'm a size 18) and some people think flaunting the flab is disgusting. It's winter now, so I'm covering up, but in the summer the amount of insults I get is huge. This is so unfair, because it's a free country and I've got just as much right as anyone else to wear what I want - size shouldn't dictate fashion, and if I want to wear a size 14 pair of combats I'll go ahead and wear them!

Also, I have few friends, because generally people aren't very accepting of my strange ways, so sometimes I feel like I'm entirely alone. People also take the piss, but that doesn't bother me as much as it used to. Actually, unless I'm in a bad mood it doesn't bother me at all, because if they choose to judge me like that it's their problem. I'm pretty familiar with it now, so I've also learnt how to ignore it - although I can't deny it's deplorable that society is so judgmental.

Editor's Note: Nita is now eighteen and I met her soon after she completed writing this book. She is a strikingly attractive young woman - lithe, slim and athletic in her movements.

Chapter 1
About Me and My Personal Opinions

Before we get started, you'll probably be interested in learning about me as a person - my likes, dislikes, opinions, views, preferences. Why am I telling you this? I'm telling you because I need to let these feelings out, and I need to clarify a few points about Asperger's syndrome. I'm telling you because everyone, at their most basic level, is at least slightly egocentric (whether they choose to admit it or not); and Asperger people are undoubtedly the most egocentric of all, although not always in a bad way.

I apologise for the excessive amount of pessimism in these views (and also throughout the entire book), but I must stress how I wrote this book to reflect the world as I saw it - be that negative or positive. I'm not always this whinging, depressed little madam, but it is a part of me that's firmly routed in my psyche, and if I try to repress it in writing then you'll never know the real me - this book is an honest Asperger account, after all.

So here are a few views of mine and how I feel they relate to my Asperger's syndrome, which will help you get to know me better:

Prejudiced school kids

Upon my last day at school I was looking at the huge wall of Year 11 student photographs, and noticed a photo of myself - a hampster-cheeked little barrel of a girl, sitting alone at a bench, one hand in a packet of crisps, the other holding an iced bun, face bearing a miserable expression. It was clear the wall wasn't being monitored, because there was a plague of scribbled writing spreading from photo to photo - obviously done by the 'in crowd'.

Peachy arse! was printed in capital letters on would-be Miss UK Anna Robertson's photo. Moped Man! was inscribed on Richard Clarkson's photo. Go on, give us a kiss! jumped out in bright red lettering from Elicia Robinson's glossy print. Then there was mine.

> ### *Get the **** out of our town and stop giving it a reputation for retards, you fat, **** witted cow!*

I felt a fire of pure anger ignite in my head. If I had been four years old I would have stamped my feet and pointed at the air and yelled until I was red in the face, but now I just stood, my eyes lingering on those cruel words that everyone else found so hilarious, as if my feet were rooted to the spot. OK, so Asperger people aren't exactly renowned for their marvellous sense of humour, but in most cases I know my jokes from my insults. With my friends it's jokes and with my enemies it's insults - and this was certainly a prime insult. That'll go down as the Pedigree Chum of the insult world, I thought to myself.

How this relates to my Asperger's syndrome:

This in-crowd think they're above everyone, and that they can dictate fashion and musical trends, the correct attitudes to have and the correct opinions to hold - pretentious egotists that they are - and they believe my Asperger's syndrome makes me inferior to them. I hate any sort of prejudice - especially towards handicapped or disabled people like myself. We are subject to the same treatment that racial immigrants used to get 40 or so years ago. In the future, I hope disabled and handicapped people are as broadly accepted as blacks and Asians are today, because no-one should be discriminated against.

Socialites

I'm not a massive fan of over-exploitative socialites (social parasites more like). These media prostitutes don't need to be specified - we all implicitly know who they are. For a start, they are blatantly talentless. Well I suppose it's what you would expect when you've never had to develop any substantial talents in order to earn money. What do these women do apart from bragging about their immeasurable wealth and fashionable exploits, and possibly the odd spot of underwear modelling? Nothing memorable that's for sure. That they could actually do anything other than this beggars belief. At least once a month, I find articles in the Sunday paper glossy supplements about these women and their blockbusting roles in new, star-studded celebrity/make-over/gossip/fashion TV shows, which really gets my goat. It's appalling - criminal even - how these anorexic ferrets of women can so easily barge their way in front of any camera with such apparent ease. They jump on the Express Television Gravy Train purely as another pathetic excuse to force-feed their trite, pampered lifestyle down our throats. Honestly, with all that money, shouldn't they be out spending instead of sauntering around a studio? Anyone with even a room-temperature IQ can see this half-a-brain-celled lunch-timer has less appeal than a plague of mosquitos in summer.

How this relates to my Asperger's syndrome:

I dislike socialites for various reasons. Firstly because I am an outcast, and they represent everything I couldn't be. Superficially, I'm jealous, but on a more truthful outlook I actually quite pity them because of their dependence on the media and their inherent principle that money leads to money. Money is not everything, glamour is not everything, reputation is not everything. Underneath it all they appear shallow and insecure. In my opinion, they are the real dependants.

Why I hate grey

A diary extract (how this relates to my Asperger's syndrome is self-explanatory):

One passion of mine is shopping. Despite rarely having enough money to buy anything (damn those calls to a mobile phone in Australia!), I can always dream, because in my mind I can pretend to be anyone... I trudge along the high street, passing people of all ages and sizes, scowling at the beauties, smiling at the beasts. I've never found it easy to relate to thin, pretty girls - and I still can't figure out why a trophy such as Kelly would want to be best friends with a walrus like me. Still, she's always been there - and when people are bonded in friendship like we are, superficiality is of no importance. My appearance doesn't matter to Kelly, but that doesn't stop it mattering to me.

Kookai beckons to me and I surrender to its force. The clothes are gorgeous, yet far too expensive for me to even contemplate buying - every Pound I earn (on the off chance that I do some work) goes on Mount Everest (a.k.a my phone bill), debts to friends (some of which have been outstanding for a whole year), and excessive amounts of junk food, junk food, and er, even more junk food! So even the reasonable price of £30 for a skimpy top far exceeds my spending ability. Take a swatch at that lavish lacey top over there - the one in that deep, rich maroon-sunset colour. I think to myself. I run my short, stubby fingers over the material, tracing the fascinating patterns with my fingertips. The biggest size in stock was 14, and I could just imagine the damage I'd do if I tried to put the garment on.

Grey, grey and more grey greets my eyes as I turn away from the lilac and maroon section. Grey suits, grey micro-minis, grey cardigans, grey hipsters, grey combat trousers... completely sick. The jungle of tenements that constitute a third of this city are mostly grey. This is an environment where everything is grey, and grey is the colour so many other people have become accustomed to living in, yet hate so much - so why any of them want to wear the colour baffles me. As I study each item of clothing, I add my own names to each shade of grey (such a flexible colour, isn't it) - bird-poop grey, prison grey, mouldy grey, I-used-to-be-black-a-very-long-time-ago grey, concrete-stairs grey, inner-city poverty grey. Yes, poverty. I feel almost neurotic about the colour, because that's what it reminds me of. Kelly always makes the most of a bad situation, and never lets any of it affect her like it does me. It's surprising that she can do this, but I, the Asperger girl who doesn't see reality the way mainstreamers do, cannot. Shouldn't it be the opposite way round? But I can never rid myself of my obsessional feelings of hate and sadness. With deprivation all around me I can't simply pretend that I'm not included within it - because I am.

Like a magnet I'm drawn to it - a lovely dark blue suit. It's impossible to take my eyes off it - the thing is gorgeous. If only they had it in a size 16 I might be able to force my flab into it. But unfortunately they don't - young women just aren't as big as they used to be... according to dressmakers. If I could have afforded it I'd go to Evans and buy one of their impressive suits, but yet again their prices are aimed at women with an income - I'm not even on £1,000! I really want a job - even selling home improvements over the phone would suffice for a while - but everywhere that offers vacancies seems to have this 'fatist' attitude. If I want to work, I want to work with no hassle from fellow employees.

I'm seething as I grimly survey the slim, attractive girls sauntering in and out of the shop. So carefree, so aloof. What I would give to be even a tiny bit like them... God... My head is burning hot, and before I know it, crippling anger has seized my thoughts and I'm narrowing my eyes contemptuously. There are times like this when all I hold for the human race is utter contempt. I'm livid because, for all my efforts, my life never goes the way I plan it. Psychologically, I reckon I've transferred some of the blame onto others in an attempt to stop pitying myself too much. It's not entirely my fault that I don't get this or that job - or that I've never had many friends - and there's a certain degree of truth in this which I cannot doubt.

I can't say though that I've never tried making friends and that I was born bitter. If anything, I've tried too hard and have been too exuberant - but constant years of bullying has moulded me into someone else.

I've become expert at disguising my true feelings, knowing that if I dare show them I'll make a complete fool of myself and be used, yet again, as a figure of fun. I've metaphorically built up a strong wall between other people and my feelings, so I can seek refuge behind it and be kept safe from abuse. This has definitely distanced me from others, but I prefer to believe that if anyone does want to know me then they'll make the effort to do so and travel that distance. So far, not many have, and I don't care at all.

Which is a lie.

A literal thought

This relates directly to my Asperger's syndrome because I'm a very literal person, to the very last degree. If I say I'll be somewhere in 3.5 minutes I'll be there in 3.5 minutes, unless something outside my control delays me. If I ask my maw (mum) to be off the phone in two minutes I expect her to be off the phone in precisely 2 minutes. Sometimes being literal is a help, but it can also be a hindrance because it pisses people off no end!

Someone once said to me that if the world was totally literal it would stop spinning, but I disagree. I don't think the world would spin any quicker if everything was as 100% literal as me, but I don't reckon it would slow down either. I think things would be noticeably different, but I couldn't say if this would be in a positive or negative way. Actually I don't reckon the world could be completely literal - there are too many factors outside our control that prevent this.

But often things annoy me when they're not as literal as I would like. For example, in the animal world partners are called 'mates'. With us humans, our partners are called our boyfriends/girlfriends, yet our friends are called our 'mates' (excluding other terms like pals and in the case of Harry Enfield, chums). It's strange, isn't it? I think so.

Conventionality verses Individuality

I don't fit under any specific labels and I don't particularly want to either. People are constantly being defined by their labels, and although bearing these labels is a form of stability - a superficial knowledge of yourself - I still don't think this is accurate.

We live under labels because they're safe - safe as in we know our social class, our dress code, the sort of people we're most likely to get along with, our musical preferences and our other interests - but all we are really doing is hiding from ourselves. We do this because we don't want to know who we really are as individuals, because basically we're afraid - afraid of being what we don't want to be, and being alienated from the crowd. So we conform. We conform because we want to fit in, or because we're too frightened to master independent thought for fear of falling out of line or acting against social conventions. I try not to categorise or generalise, but sometimes it's inevitable - it's a character flaw most of us share. And in this case it's necessary, because it's far simpler splitting society into two categories - those who conform and those who don't - than treating everyone as an individual. Unless you are only comparing two distinct people (for example, the President of the US and Scotland's First Minister) then you're very likely to be dealing with large groups, and individual comparisons would just cause a disorderly mess.

It's easy to fall under the misconception that everyone within a certain category is of the same mentality, especially if you've had a certain experience with a few of them - for example, 'anyone who is into Marilyn Manson is a devil worshipper' (not true). It's even easier to be misconceived if you've got Asperger's syndrome as, until I was 12, I had a tendency to categorise everything, perceiving everyone in that category as clones of each other. Even though generic cloning is often inaccurate where the individual is concerned, it's definitely closer to the truth for particular groups within it. For example, a group of friends who all support their home football team, and all frequent the same local pubs and clubs, could be branded loyal or unadventurous. A group of friends who share a passion for computers could wither be branded geeks. But is it essential to have something in common with someone? It certainly makes it easier to relate to them and always provides a topic of mutual interest, but what if your personality clashes with theirs despite this? I like the same Sheffield Hard House club as a lot of people, but I don't get along with all of them. A shared interest brings us together but does not necessarily unite us. Plus, there's truth in the theory that opposites attract and alikes repel, because I have nothing in common with my friend James and we've got a marvellous friendship.

Just how important is it to be popular and conform to the standards of a group? And how taboo is it to be a loner? If you've always been the gregarious, popular type, then having an army of friends and admirers could easily become your staple in life. On the other hand, if you prefer your own, or little company, then popularity may be irrelevant to you. If you are desperate to fit in with others, then conformity, despite how oppressive, could be a useful strategy for you - one which you could well become dependent on. If, however, you are an independent person with a strong sense of your own identity, then you could see conformity as trivial.

How this relates to my Asperger's syndrome:

I've tried to conform, with little success. Conforming didn't make me any more normal and has only ever given me grief. After years of fighting a losing battle, I eventually opted for the alternative rather than the conventional, which was the only way I could arrive at an acceptance of myself. Conformity is not the right way for everyone and this is nothing to be ashamed of. I've learned that, with a number of Asperger people, trying to be someone that you're not is impossible - which is why some find acting and role-play so challenging.

Having this syndrome denotes our difference from the start, so we find conformity a much harder task than most. So the only solution, I believe, is not to conform. You've got to accept yourself for who you are - however tough this may be. Being in denial will only hinder you. Acknowledge your syndrome, research it, and remember that anyone who is unkind to you because of your difference isn't worth it in the first place. That is easier said than done I know - I'm not completely there yet! Accepting yourself, therefore, is the key to personal success - if I hadn't accepted myself then I would never have written this book. The only person who can make you accept yourself is you and you alone; so realise that wearing an orange hat in a sea of green ones is perfectly OK. If conformity clashes with you then don't conform - it might disrupt your life in the short-term, but will improve it in the long-term. And, most importantly, be true to yourself, because ultimately, you only have yourself to depend on.

Expressing myself (this is directly related to my Asperger's syndrome)

It is a common myth that Asperger people are generally somewhat distanced from the world, or unfeeling, withdrawn or introverted. This is not to say that we don't or can't possess opinions and emotions of our own; quite the contrary in fact. Just because we express ourselves in a different way to mainstream people does not mean that we do not experience the same emotions, or hold any particular views on the world. We are not intrinsically different from mainstreamers.

Other Asperger people I know have quite profound opinions on various things - it is a simple fact that many of us do not feel we have the confidence, right, or legitimate forum in which to voice them - so we stay mute. I may not be particularly clever or skilled with words, but that doesn't mean I don't have the same feelings as everyone else. I'm not overly articulate, so it's not exactly easy to express myself on the page. But I try, and that's the best I can do.

Another reason we do not always express ourselves as fluently as mainstreamers is because we don't have the ability. We are already impeded (yes, I do mean impeded) by our inability to interact and communicate in a social context. For some of us it is difficult to voice our opinions because we cannot translate our thoughts into words - we may try but the result is often a babbled splurge or an unrehearsed mess - like performers with stage fright.

Until I left secondary school that was always the case with me. So what did I do to rectify my predicament? Simple: I rehearsed what I was thinking of saying to the extent that I felt my words were somehow contrived, or artificially constructed to suit the occasion. However, I experienced many teething problems with this method. For a start, I actually talked as if I was reading from a script, despite trying to appear spontaneous, which only isolated me more. Over time, I've managed to apply the method properly and convince others that I can have a spontaneous reaction like them. The only one who knows my secret is me. As with acting, speed and timing is compulsory, so I've had to learn how to think quickly and respond without a hitch - and this isn't easy.

Every conversation is still a struggle for me, but I know that eventually I won't need to rehearse my lines any more. I listen intently to other people's conversations and make mental notes, and because I'm actually listening, I'm also learning. Right now I'm acting, but in effect everyone is an actor - they tell lies, they exaggerate, they fantasise, they front. OK, so their act is a totally separate play - mine is with forming conversation, theirs is with the content of the conversation - but a film star and someone who dresses up as Santa for the children's grotto, are effectively still doing the same thing. Acting is acting, no matter what the context.

Editor's Note: When I met Nita she was speaking with a strong Glaswegian accent. When she sang she used a West Coast American accent. She gave a me a demonstration of her various voices, but I did not hear Nita's own voice.

You've Heard the Rumours, But Are They True? Preconceptions of Asperger's Syndrome

Common myth 1: stupidity

Asperger's syndrome and learning difficulties are not mutually exclusive - I am living proof of that. I learn at a much slower pace than most people, and if I had £1 for every time I had been branded a complete dunce, then I'd be a millionaire by now. I try just as hard to learn, I work just as hard, I channel as much effort as I can into my studies - yet it all amounts to the grand total of 'what the hell's this? Are you completely retarded?!' This is why I have written this book - to set the record straight about the problems frequently associated with Asperger's syndrome. Learning difficulties are common with Asperger youngsters, but this is not to say we are incompetent. Consider the incredible talent of Einstein in science, Donna Williams (author of the critically-acclaimed *Nobody Nowhere* and *Somebody Somewhere*) and Clare Sainsbury (author of the award-winning *Martian in the Playground*) for literature, and possibly even Shakespeare and Bill Gates, then you've got evidence that Asperger's syndrome does not equate with stupidity.

If anything, Asperger people are exceptionally gifted in some form or other. Every Asperger person I know is talented in at least one area, but this is sometimes repressed because of their lack of confidence. So Asperger youngsters are best encouraged in their talents; the worst thing you can do is allow them to hide their light under a bushel. Congratulate them on their gifts, and never fail to remind them that they have something special which no-one can ever take from them. If the youngster is already being taunted then this is imperative because it might help build some confidence and self-esteem. This way, Asperger children can develop and apply their talents with determination and pride. Let them pursue what they want - don't enforce your own hopes and dreams onto them because they will only resent you for it. Give them the independence to choose their own path, then provide them with all the hope and encouragement they need to help them through.

Ever since I was at junior school I've loved art. There was no better stress reliever for me than slopping paint all over a sheet of paper and making a thorough mess of my hands and overalls. My passion for art was bullied into submission (along with drama and music) until the last two years of secondary school, when I decided to let one aspect of my character shine through. And I'm so glad I did. When my whole personality was repressed, I had almost convinced myself that I was a hopeless case in every way - and if I had continued like that I don't think I would have even attempted college. When my family and I gave me that encouragement, I excelled in art and passed the course with top marks (modesty can take a back seat for once!). I hope this is an inspiration to any other aspiring Asperger artists.

Common myth 2: problems with imagination

(from Lorna Wing's *Triad of Impairments*)

Call me slack, but I lifted this quote from Clare Sainsbury's *Martian in the Playground*' (Lucky Duck Publishing, 2000, Bristol) because I couldn't have put this description better myself:

> *"The... (problems with imagination), term is somewhat misleading, as it doesn't mean 'lack of imagination' in a conventional sense. Some children and adults with Asperger's syndrome can be highly imaginative as the term is usually understood, developing elaborate fantasy worlds. Instead it is more useful to think of this element of the triad in terms of problems with flexible thinking, leading to problems coping with change and a need for rigid routines, and difficulty imagining what other people may be thinking."*

An example of this problem comes from my childhood, when I would devise routines for myself, in order to gain some control over my life. At age 10, I was setting my alarm clock for 5:30 am, then I would allow myself half an hour to eat breakfast, then another half-hour to get washed and dressed. Then, bizarrely, I would go back to sleep until 8 am, after which I would get up and go to school, with crumpled clothing and ragged hair (and I always wondered why the other kids called me a tramp!). If my alarm didn't go off, and I woke up, say, 10 minutes later than usual, I would feel completely lost and out of control. If there weren't any cornflakes in the cupboard, and I had to eat toast for breakfast (which took less time), I would go ballistic. Six slices of toast only took me 10 minutes to eat, whereas three huge bowls of cereal would take me half an hour. What I was going to do with that extra 20 minutes was completely unfathomable, too much to bear thinking about. When I went back to bed I refused to get up until my alarm started ringing. If my mother said we had to leave early, I would go ape, because that would mean altering my routine. This routine of mine had to be **absolutely precise** - period.

I also had immense difficulty imagining what other people might be thinking, but up until my diagnosis the thought didn't even cross my mind. Once I knew what was wrong with me, I read up on my condition and came across this thing called personal insight, which I was told I could use to assess myself. Now I knew I had this strange ability, I thought I might as well implement it. So I took a step back and sort of assessed myself.

I discovered that I couldn't comprehend people's facial expressions, what they said or the way in which they said it. Reminiscing on my early school days I realised how I used to laugh when someone cried because I thought the other person was laughing. I can't understand how I made this mistake - all I know is that I did it often. Similarly, when I broke something at school and the teacher told me off, I couldn't understand why she was addressing me in such loud, frightening words. When kids at school had arguments and upset each other, I couldn't understand why some didn't speak to each other for a while, why some cried, why some flaunted such weird facial expressions. This terrified me and made me feel even more of an alien than before. At least prior to diagnosis, I was blissfully ignorant of many of my problems. It's as though I was speaking an alien language, except that I wasn't aware of it. Then suddenly I discovered that I had been speaking this other language all my life and I had to learn the one the rest of society was speaking. It was more daunting than you could ever imagine.

Common myth 3: disliking change

This follows directly on from the previous common myth, and is certainly true to some extent. I depend on routine and structure in my life because it helps me put things into perspective and prevents me from losing my balance. If my routine and structure is altered, I find myself phased and unable to cope. So yes, in this sense I dislike change. However, change doesn't just apply to one area of life - such as a change in routine or structure - it can associate itself with everything. For example, there can be change in scenery, personality, the five senses - everything - and in fact, some of these changes would actually be welcomed. This is explained in this diary extract, which I wrote on the bus on the way to college:

I use the bus journey to and from college as a time to reflect. Out of the corner of my eye, I study the haggard face of the woman from Pine Close. Her hair is long and unkempt, her cheeks are hollow, her eyes are rimmed with red from many sleepless nights, and her clothes are faded and worn - this woman is only 30, yet I wouldn't put 47 past her. Her five-year-old son usually accompanies her, but today her grandfather is here instead...It pains me to look at her every day and see her slowly deteriorating. Sounds patronising, I know, but I feel so sorry for her. My frustration multiplies like cancerous cells every time she boards the bus in the morning, her state worse than the day before. This could be a Ken Loach drama, or possibly even a *Trainspotting*-esque British blockbuster of sorts: 'It's got the grit of reality, the depravation of the inner-city, the self-annihilation of those without a future... yes, it's Nita's Journey On The Bus! (fabulous rounds of applause).

Then there's the old couple from no. 93 - the bungalow - (get this: they moved there from no. 64 in 1993, after the previous owner had died, aged 93. Now they're both steadily approaching 93... spooky) with their zimmer-frames and their Jack Russel. Those beige coats that they always wear urgently require a visit to the cleaners - as they have done for a good few months now. There's the 20-something with her baby - she always alights two stops before town to go to her work at the crèche. A trio of girls from the estate are slouched across the back seat, chatting and guffawing over the incident in the local pub last night. God, how much do I hate them?! How much do I hate their disorderly banter at 8:05 in the bloody morning - and their recollections of the terrific night before?! Yes, OK, so I'm jealous - so what? If I didn't know these people it would be alright. If I didn't know they were out every night, partying and pulling and cruising the streets in their boyfriend's modified cars, then I wouldn't care. But I went to school with them and they ripped the piss outa me, so there's no way I can ever forget them. I need a change of scenery, like NOW! I'm so bored with seeing the same old things over and over again. The longer I stay here and the more familiar I am with it, the more I view it with contempt. I'm getting so claustrophobic in this town now, having been here so long - too long. Everyday here is a day too much. Every hour here is an hour of monotony.

And I'm writing with blue biro again. Time to change to pink me thinx.

Chapter 2
School, Bullying, and Being Manipulated

Alien

A wry smile passes round
the room, who
are you talking
to?
Who are you looking
at?
I don't understand
your eyes

and mouths
are a mystery to me.
When you laugh and when you
smile
and
snigger
and
fool
around with each other.

I hate your words, they
make me cringe
and
inwardly shudder.
Always the same.
Always the same.
For want of a better...

Outcast

I was always the outcast at school - the friendless retard with an imaginary dunces cap super-glued to my bulbous head. I got so used to being called spastic and freak that I even replied to them instead of my real name. Later on in life, the inventory of names broadened to grease pit, crater face, seaweed hair, Mrs Blobby, among various other obscenities too crude to reveal ('Oh go on!' I hear you cry). Looking back I am able to laugh at the latter two not-so-obscene ones but, believe me, I've never been able to look at seaweed or Mr Blobby in the same way again!

School terrified me. So much so that when I was there, I locked myself in a toilet cubicle at break and lunch times. The other kids knew my hiding place and often ambled into the toilets to turn on all the taps at full blast, flush the other cubicles and bang on the doors, throw the soaps at the ceiling, whilst yelling obscenities at me. And how would I react? I'd crouch on the floor, cowering in terror, clutching at my rolls of fat for desperate comfort - whimpering. Ritual humiliation almost became an expected part of my life, and I cringe just reminiscing.

Alternative idol

I'll never forget the stench of rotten banana and PVC glue that haunted the toilets, or the sheer amount of bubble gum - and soggy toilet paper (no lie!) - stuck to the ceiling. To fill the time I spent just standing or crouching in that freezing cubicle, I'd often count the bubble gum pieces, and wonder just how the scrunched-up loo roll stayed up there.

One day, curiosity got the better of me, and I pulled off a huge hand full of loo roll and emerged from my claustrophobic heaven into the big bad sink area to dampen the tissue, squeeze the excess moisture out then hurl the soggy lump upwards. To my amazement it stuck. And it stayed. Every time I was in the toilets I'd check to see it was still there, because it was the only form of permanence I had. Silly, this, but I placed all my faith in it, and in my head transformed an inanimate object into my own personal symbol of stability. Oh well, Christians had crucifixes, Buddhists had statues of Buddha; and I had a scrunched-up, dried-up thing fixed to greying plaster. Each to their own, I suppose. Maybe it's still there.

Popping the cherry

I lost my virginity young, but not because I had conceded. The incident had happened when I was 13, when this rowdy boy had been dared by pals to screw the ugliest bird in town. He didn't exactly rape me because I was practically away with the fairies at the time, and didn't have a scooby doo what I was doing. When the realisation hit me, I just sat back, shut my mouth and let myself be taken advantage of. Why? Because I thought this was the only chance I'd ever get to lose my virginity - because when you had been labelled Loch Ness Monster and Beast of Bodmin, boys weren't exactly queuing up to have sex with you.

I thought this would be my first and last sexual encounter, so I might as well submit to it. Although, secretly, I knew it wasn't what I wanted, or what I deserved.

Also, I lacked that vital self-confidence to resist. After all, I was nothing but a short, fat, pathetic weakling, whose purpose in life was to be the butt of everyone's jokes. It seemed as though all my peers had active sex lives, and being the extremely naive kid that I was (13 years old but with a mentality of eight), the notion that time was slipping through my fingers at a rate of knots, coupled with the overwhelming pressure to conform, compelled me to do the wrong thing.

But when I eventually realised that I had been used yet again as a figure of fun, I didn't show my face in town for weeks. Since then my confidence became extinct when it comes to the opposite sex. Even though I knew it was true that no-one would ever go out with me, I couldn't deny my natural emotions - there were boys I lusted after, and yet I knew they wouldn't touch me with a barge pole. It seemed as though I was marred by disaster after disaster. Wherever I was, trouble would seek me out and grab me. Oh well, if some people are born blessed, some are also born tainted!

Fantasy

Despite being a loser in every sense, I maintained a belief that somehow I'd get my revenge. I devised elaborate plots, detailing how I'd do this. I drew pictures, I wrote stories. In my fantasy life I was victorious, courageous, strong and popular. I intended to achieve this by the time I reached my teens.

But the courage never arrived, and my planned revenge never happened. Thirteen came miserably, and went, with me still a loner and a pathetic weakling, easily suppressed by the bullies and subservient to their demands - mute and grovelling like some unworthy slave to her master's feet. I felt like less of a person and more of a corpulent object to be abused. Half the time I was nothing more than a physical entity - a lump of big-boned, ugly lardfat - nothing more. I felt like I had no right to be anything other than a 'thing' or an 'it'. Of course, the bullying was initiated by my evidently abnormal behaviour, and not my weight; but the weight was always a problem nonetheless. The bullies recognised the difference instantly and labelled me as freak and weird. I had the personality of a slug on valium, never uttering a word to my peers except 'sorry'. I actually didn't feel worthy to be liked.

Unaware

At the time, I wasn't aware just how unusual it seemed - because I didn't think I was actually all that abnormal. Eccentric maybe, but certainly not abnormal. I didn't recognise anything strange about gibbering on about one particular thing repetitively. I didn't realise talking to myself indicated madness, or that my constant twitching looked so freakish, or that my chosen style of walking like I was about to topple over was anything out of the ordinary. That was the problem with my Asperger's syndrome - I didn't know just how different I was, because I couldn't read the signs. I didn't understand my peers' reactions to my behaviour, so instead of reflecting on their reactions and asking myself why they seemed so incomprehensible, I just forgot about the whole thing and continued as always.

Being manipulated

Another cringe-worthy memory is how effortlessly I could be manipulated, and consequently how my peers wound me up for their own comedic purposes. It wasn't exactly difficult to get me to humiliate myself, because I was provoked by the most trivial of things. In the last year of primary school, someone wrote 'Boo' on my maths book and I flew into a mad rage - running riot around the classroom bawling my eyes out, yelling how someone was trying to scare me and how I wanted to go home. If I wasn't allowed home then I would go and stand in one corner of the room facing the wall, stamping my feet and shaking my head and gesticulating maniacally. The other pupils found my show hilarious, and would all sit about watching me make a bigger and bigger prat of myself. I really was like some grotesque form of clockwork doll or a puppet on a string - and the most stupid thing was, I was blind to it.

The manipulation process repeated itself at secondary school, but in different ways. I've always been a sucker for food (which is one of the reasons why I'm overweight), and the other kids in my form would often leave a unopened bag of crisps, a cream bun or a packet of sweets on the table nearest door, so when I passed by I would spot the food and, believing the room was deserted (and being too naive to smell the air of conspiracy), I would bumble on in, irrespective of the matter of germs or the possibility that the food belonged to someone else. All I knew was that I could see FOOD and I HAD TO HAVE FOOD NOW!

I would reach the table, drop my two-tonne bag (I used to bring books for every lesson each day because I could never remember my timetable, plus a huge dictionary, thesaurus, and a hoard of library books; along with a packed lunch and the extra few rolls, cans of fizzy drink, chocolate bars and packets of crisps that I had bought for snacks between lessons) on the floor and suddenly, a large group of my peers would burst out of the store cupboard, grab the food out of my hands and smear it on my face and in my hair, whilst spitting at me and pelting me with soggy chewing gum, and tipping sachets of pepper and salt over my head. Then they'd sprint off, leaving me huddling under a table, sobbing, whimpering, rocking back and forth, too terrified to run to a teacher.

You'd think that, after the first incident, I would have alerted myself and become more cautious - that I wouldn't allow myself to be lured into the same trap again - but no. It had to happen three times before I actually realised the pattern. Unfortunately, as soon as I had figured this out, the other kids unleashed plan B. They would approach me - the short, timid fat girl - at break time, saying how guilty they felt for taunting me and asking me to accept a seemingly unopened packet of crisps, can of fizzy drink or bag of chips as a token of apology. They would stand around while I reached into the bag of crisps (which I suddenly noticed were already open but thought nothing more of it) or chips, shoved a huge handful into my mouth and chomped...and chomped until I suddenly noticed a tingling sensation inside my mouth. The tingling sensation grew and before I knew it my whole mouth was burning - the kids had sprinkled the crisps or chips with hellishly spicy curry powder.

But it was the cans of drink that were worst. The bullies would put ants, worms, maggots or even wasps in the drinks. Fortunately, I never got stung by the wasps, but I did swallow a few ants, maggots and worms. I can honestly say that I'm one of the few lucky people to also know what a Tizer *avec* vinegar cocktail, a Coca-Cola *avec* paint shake and Slush Puppie *avec* tiny shards of plastic bonanza, taste like! I can't believe how I managed to fall for this trick every single time! I suppose it was because I was always raised with the Christian concept of turning the other cheek , and because I honestly sustained too much faith in the power of good triumphing over evil. I believed my tormentors would either repent or be struck down in almighty vengeance, and that I would be saved.

Prevention is sometimes better than cure

Sadly, I'm not the only Asperger person to have experienced these problems; the majority of the Asperger population have suffered similar things, and like me, most have not realised just how abnormal they are until they were being victimised - too frightened to defend themselves. It appears that this is an inevitable cycle most Asperger children go through. But it isn't always necessary to learn the hard way, so how can this cycle be prevented?

If the Asperger child has been diagnosed before starting school, then it is relatively simple (although nothing is ever truly simple where Asperger people are concerned). Talk to the child about her condition, inform her of everything she should know about it, but don't pressure her to attempt to behave like the mainstream children. This could result in feelings of guilt - the child believing it's 'wrong' to have Asperger's syndrome, making her even more susceptible to the jibes of others and leading to deeper self-hatred.

Try to inform the teachers of the child's condition, making the rest of the class aware that the eccentric or introverted kid in the corner is not insane. I can't guarantee anyone will listen (especially the classmates), but it is important that you visit the school yourself and explain every intricate detail of your child's condition. You can't be there every time she behaves strangely (you'd never be able to leave her side if you lived by that principle!), so someone at school has to understand.

You could maybe try obtaining a teaching assistant to support the Asperger child and help explain to classmates about the condition. However, you should only consider this if you know the child won't feel self-conscious, because enforcing a guardian on someone who doesn't want one can do more harm than good.

If the child is already at school, friendless and victimised, I would suggest trying to explain the condition to the teachers and classmates, and if this proves to be of no benefit, then sending the child to another school, or removing the child from school altogether and teaching her at home. This depends on your resources, your financial situation, and how much time you can afford to spare. My mother had to sacrifice her job in order to try teaching me at home, which was a very admirable thing to do considering money has always been a difficult issue for us. She then had to find part-time evening work so as to get me two hours of tuition a week, and every night she would come back completely fatigued. Those last two years of school were some of the hardest we've ever endured - financially, physically and psychologically.

But we can't all be saints, so don't reprimand yourself if devoting more time or money to your child isn't possible - because it's not your fault. Hopefully, by the time you've read this, my mother's dream - to open a school and private tuition service for Asperger children will be underway - fingers, toes and eyeballs crossed.

It is unfortunate that some Asperger people don't exactly embrace the syndrome with open arms; they are in denial. I'm no psychologist or psychoanalyst or whatever the term is, but I can hazard a few guesses as to why some are in denial. They might feel that accepting their condition will brand them or set them apart from the rest of the population (not true). They might prefer to do an ostrich - bury their heads in the sand, in the hope that ignoring Asperger's syndrome will eliminate it (also not true).

It is important to understand and accept that Asperger's syndrome is a life-long condition, and no amount of distraction can make it go away. It is also important to remember that the syndrome is relatively invisible upon first sight - in that I mean that you cannot point out an Asperger person, say, walking down the street. You don't set eyes on someone and instantly know they have Asperger's syndrome. It's certainly true that a number of Asperger people have strange mannerisms (people have told me I've got a strange walk), but you usually can't detect an Asperger person simply from appearances alone. The syndrome is visible through what they say, and do and how they say and do things.

Because Asperger people can be exceptionally stubborn when they get the chance, denial can pose a big problem. The less they acknowledge their condition, the less they can improve upon their social skills, and consequently the higher the probability of them being friendless and/or victimised. Don't think that acknowledgement solves everything (it doesn't), but at least it brings a certain amount of self-awareness, which can be built upon. Once the Asperger person has this acknowledgement, learning the tricks of the trade - or the rules of the game, as some people refer to it - will be feasible, providing they are advised and directed by people who have at least a basic understanding of the syndrome.

Schools and colleges - to mainstream or not to mainstream?

With every Asperger youngster, it is important to consider their educational needs far above those of mainstream kids. In my experience, most mainstream kids aren't really bothered about which school/college they attend - as long as they're with their pals they're OK. Asperger kids are different; fundamentally because quite a few of them don't have any friends to begin with - and are neither self-sufficient (by that I mean finding their way around without getting confused) nor self-confident. The prospect of starting a new school or college can be extremely daunting. Some thrive on solitude and would be best taught alone; some feel more secure in a protected environment with others like themselves and some want to be in mainstream education because it makes them feel more normal. Sometime these kids or their families are in denial.

The Asperger youngster shouldn't be forced to attend a special school because this will only discourage learning. It's a tough situation though - you might be certain that special schooling would be beneficial, but your son/daughter opposes it. In my honest opinion, in this event, forgo your own ideas of what is in your child's best interest, and let him/her to make the decision. If it all backfires then you can review the situation again, and maybe plan a change.

If your child is undecided about which sort of school to go to, then weigh out the pros and cons of mainstream education, private tuition or special schooling. In mainstream schools the majority of Asperger kids stick out like a sore thumb, and are made to feel like freaks by their peers. This only hinders their ability to learn. On the other hand, some Asperger kids might sail through mainstream school/college on the strength of their intelligence alone, irrespective of the taunts they might receive. Or some might be the class joker. Mainstream education isn't necessarily all bad - it just depends on the individual.

In mainstream college I found a wider variety of students, but variety doesn't always solve everything. In my experience, all groups can be equally discriminating. I don't fit in anywhere at college. I'm not clever enough to be a boffin and not dumb enough to be a dunce. I'm certainly not trendy, but I'm not a goth, grunger or cartoon character. I'm not shy enough to be considered meek, but I'm not confident enough to be considered, er, confident. A few of my Asperger friends go to, and have attended, special colleges, and their fees were paid by their local education authorities, some with positive results, others with not so positive. One friend said he detested his special college because of the stigma attached to it - he felt as though it branded him disabled. However, another friend's opinion was totally different, she enjoyed a college in which she didn't feel oppressed by the other students. Personally, I wouldn't have wanted to go to a special college, simply because I want to learn how to interact with mainstreamers in a mainstream environment. OK, admittedly this hasn't all gone according to plan, but I'm still persevering with it nonetheless. And yes, I appreciate that I can't really talk - because I dropped out of school - but at least now I'm trying.

The other alternative is home tuition, but everyone knows this has a major catch. It's expensive and good home tutors are scarce. My local education authority only funded two hours a week for me, and my mother had to pay the rest. She had to work two jobs to afford it, and to pay the rent and rates, and we struggled. If you have enough money to afford a home tutor then fine, but if you don't then I can't pretend it'll be easy.

Home tuition was the best method for me, because I could directly relate to the tutor, with no jeers and distractions from other students. I could also take my time (although extra time meant extra money), and because of this I managed to learn masses more than if I had been in a classroom situation.

To summarise, assess the pros and cons, according to the individual. Advise your child on what you think is best, but respect their own opinion and support the decision s/he makes, whatever the outcome. And if home tuition is the best option, then badger the hell out of your LEA!

My mother's recommendations for teaching Asperger students:
1) Asperger students find change difficult. There should be prior warnings - both written and verbal - for any changes in timetables, teachers or classrooms. Failure to do so could result in anxiety and apprehension and the student's reluctance to learn.

2) Monitor your language. You should speak clearly and in simple, unambiguous terms. Asperger students can get confused very easily by metaphors, irony, sarcasm or idiomatic speech.

3) Insistence on understanding is essential. You cannot afford to be complacent where Asperger students are concerned. Don't assume they will learn like mainstreamers, or be able to follow instructions. It is crucial that the Asperger student understands in order to progress. I would advise repeating the instructions at least twice, or giving them in writing. It could be suggested that you separate each instruction, number it and write it on a piece of coloured card - a different colour for each instruction - that could make it easier to remember. Although writing everything down can get tedious, it will eliminate a lot of future stress.

4) Most teachers now accept that a tape recorder is an invaluable resource for Asperger students who have trouble taking notes. Lectures/lessons can then be recorded and played back in the student's free time. In my opinion, this creates an almost hassle-free approach to learning. It certainly requires more time, but I believe it's worth it if it helps the student work successfully.

5) Where Asperger students are having academic difficulties, the teacher should devote some time after the lesson - or as soon after the lesson as possible - to clarify any problems the student might have. This should be on a one to one basis and in a quiet place.

6) Asperger students can be easily distracted, so, before giving any instructions, address the student directly (by name or a tap on the shoulder) to be certain you have their full attention. To keep their attention, reinforce any instructions, and if the student is not adverse to being singled out, ask if any help is needed.

7) Many Asperger students are perfectionists, or have trouble organising their thoughts, so will need extra time to complete the work. If they suffer from handwriting problems, or maybe where proximity to their peers causes them stress, allowing them access to a computer or laptop might be a solution.

8) Asperger students may not be motivated to work - showing reluctance in an activity that they are not personally interested in. A creative teacher might be able to build the lesson around the Asperger student's particular interest, so it is important beforehand to engage in informal conversation with the student and to be familiar with their likes and dislikes.

9) Group work can be a problem, so it is not uncommon for Asperger students to prefer working on their own. This might be because they rely on their own ideas before anyone else's, and in a group situation, where most things require

give and take, they would have to forego some of their own ideas. To an Asperger student who insists his/her own ideas are paramount, the desire to be boss and to dominate the decision can override the consideration for other people's ideas. On the other hand, the student might be too shy and afraid of others to contribute any ideas, or too phased/distracted by the amount of noise around, so the only way to work would be to sit alone.

10) Organisation is an important issue to consider. Asperger students require a lot more time to organise themselves, so never fail to notify them early about when to clear up and put their coat on. Some Asperger students are organised to a T, yet others can be incredibly messy, creating chaos all around them. These are the Asperger students most likely to forget and lose things, so always allow them ample time to check they've got everything before they leave the lesson. They are also likely to forget to bring simple things like pens and pencils to school, so keep an inventory of these things for when this happens.

11) A contentious matter is whether or not to tell the student's peers about his/her condition. In my honest opinion, I believe both options have their pros and cons. Educating the peers on the subject would certainly sort the friends from the enemies, but this is just as likely to occur over time anyway. Bigoted classmates might alienate or bully the student if they are informed of his/her syndrome, but compassionate ones (if there are any) might feel endeared to the student. In some cases, explaining the condition to the classmates could actually prevent bullying and instead promote and encourage tolerance.

12) Many Asperger students suffer from low self-esteem. This might be mitigated by assigning them to a specific job or role within the classroom, which could help them feel special and responsible, with a sense of purpose. Even basic tasks like opening and closing windows, turning on the lights, cleaning the board and stacking the chairs can be worthwhile.

13) Never fail to praise the Asperger students when they get something right, instead of punishing them when they get something wrong. I can't think of a more PC way to phrase this, but in this respect, about 50% of Asperger students can be treated in a very similar way to dogs (this is in no way meant to sound derogatory) - they can be trained to work well. Like dogs, they respond better to a system of rewards rather than punishments, so always reward them - maybe with a small gift at break time, if they want to avoid being teacher's pet.

14) It's very easy to distract and distress Asperger students. Their highly developed sensory awareness can amplify certain environmental factors; such as the buzzing of fluorescent lights, the squeaking of pens on the whiteboard, chalk

on the blackboard, creaking of floors, army of voices, uncomfortable clothing, room temperature, amount of classroom activity and/or visual stimuli, too little personal space/ invasion of privacy. The student might become overwhelmed and confused by everything, which could result in anxiety or aggressive outbursts. The teacher could maybe remove the student from the classroom to the library, or even provide earplugs so the student does not drown in all the classroom noise.

15) The Asperger student is best seated away from distractions - maybe at the front of the class, end of a row, or near the teacher. This makes it easier for contact with the teacher, and therefore simplifies the task of gaining the student's attention. They should never be placed in the middle of the room, because being at the centre of everything could make them an easy target for all-round bullying, confusion and distraction, amongst other things.

16) Asperger students rarely conform, and consequently they can't be treated the same as their mainstream peers. Life is like a game, with unspoken rules to be followed, but Asperger students don't realise this; therefore the teachers will require truckloads of patience and tolerance if they are to remain in control of the situation. This might not be easy, but it's got to be done. Allowances have to be made, which other classmates might see as unfair, but if they are well-informed of Asperger's syndrome and its implications, then they will hopefully be more accepting. Bullying, jibing and scapegoating are all too common in Asperger students' lives, and the teacher will have to remain vigilant in correcting this. If they don't, the Asperger student could be put off education for life.

17) Some Asperger students can find rules puzzling and illogical. It would help to discuss the school/college rules with them. Because many Asperger students are excessively curious, give them reasons for the rules - such as why certain behaviours are unacceptable, what impact they have on others, and what sanctions should be placed on the offender. Don't just bombard them with reasons, discuss them, asking frequently if they understand.

18) At times of anxiety and stress, it is essential that the student has somewhere else to go for respite. Staying in the classroom with the plethora of peers and tasks is never the answer, because it will only distress the student more. Any disruption caused by removing the student from the classroom will be much less than keeping them in there. It is equally important to remember that this should also be the case at break and lunch times, when the Asperger student's inept attempts at socialisation often render them as the butt of jokes and

bullying. It goes without saying that Asperger students are more vulnerable in unstructured times.

19) Some Asperger students might refuse to co-operate. Insistence on conformity could generate power struggles. If the behaviour is just odd and doesn't really involve anyone else, then it is best to ignore it, and hopefully the peer group will persuade the student. If, however, the peer group won't help, or the Asperger student's behaviour threatens the functioning of the classroom, the student should be removed from the classroom and brought to their place of respite to cool off. It's got to be made clear that rowdy behaviour won't be tolerated, but this should be said in a calm, advisory tone rather than a raised voice. Give the student a chance to tell their side of the story though, because they might have been provoked by a peer.

20) Inappropriate sexual behaviour is often the result of curiosity, the need for attention, or hostility towards someone who might have rejected the Asperger student; but it is most frequently due to social naivete. Asperger students often feel the same sexual urges as mainstream students, but don't realise the effect their unwanted advances can have on others. The teacher should discuss with them what is and isn't acceptable.

Making sense of Asperger students - some things teachers should know:

1) Tendency to learn set solutions to a problem and then apply them to every situation.

2) All or nothing way of thinking. Difficulty comprehending illogical or abstract concepts, or estimating roughly.

3) Good verbal skills are often merely a parroting back of something they have heard or read, and can disguise poor comprehension. Don't assume they understand all that they say.

4) Asperger students learn theory easily, but can have difficulty putting it into practice.

5) They can be very literal. For example, if you say 'wait a minute', they will count 60 seconds.

6) Because many Asperger students lack imagination, they can have considerable difficulty in sequencing and predicting; they find it hard to understand cause and effect. They should be taught slowly and with lots of repetition.

7) Asperger students have trouble reading facial expressions, interpreting body language and tone of voice. Many have limited eye contact, not due to shyness, but because faces contain too much information to process simultaneously. This, however, can be learned over time.

8) They can be clumsy (many are dyspraxic and well as dyslexic), poorly co-ordinated physically, and regularly lack common sense.
9) They have a continuing inability to form successful relationships.
10) They can get extremely anxious, nervous, frustrated and confused about the simplest of things. Things that are trivial to mainstreamers can be very stressful or confusing to Asperger students.

Teachers who gave me a chance

Throughout my life I've been reprimanded by teachers and students alike for being weird, uncooperative, stupid, weak, forgetful, slow - the list is endless. However, there have been a number of teachers who have tried their best to understand and support me, and I really feel they deserve a mention. Also, because my condition separates me from my peers, I have often found friendship in adults of the 30+ age, who don't misjudge me like people of my own age do. My fellow students taunted me for being teacher's pet, but that just goes with the territory. Of course it upset me, but what else could I do? Be absolutely friendless in class?

At school there was Mr Osbourne in my Music class, Mr Doughty in Maths, and Mrs Taylor in French. These teachers always made time for me, despite me whinging to them every spare moment about my problems. Mr Osbourne was always bubbly and ready to make a light-hearted joke out of anything. He rarely got angry or raised his voice like most of my other teachers did. He let me hide in the music department's store cupboard at break time, without even blinking an eye, it was as though he understood and accepted why I needed to go to ridiculous measures to separate myself from society. I respected him for not probing for answers like everyone else did. Occasionally he would tap on the door, say 'boo!' and offer me a biscuit (which I never declined). On the last day of term, I bought him a tin of biscuits in return for the amount of biscuity yumminess he had allowed me.

Stephen Rea look-alike Mr Doughty was a sensitive soul with a fighter's personality. He was straightforward and brutally honest, always giving as good as he got, yet he was never afraid to show his vulnerable side. He'd been through, and was still going through, a lot, and if it got to him then he wouldn't hide it; but he never missed a class, and he never gave in. I admired him so much, and aspired to be the sort of enduring, determined person that he was. The other kids would mock him and belittle his predicament when they knew full well it was no laughing matter. I felt as if I was the only pupil who cared. He also allowed me to take refuge in his (sadly) biscuitless office at registration time, and didn't go ape when I raided his banana stash time and time again.

When a pupil stole his Maths Bible, I bought him a new one. Mr Doughty was furiously passionate about his subject, constantly mentioning how this book was God to all mathematicians, and how even as a qualified teacher he couldn't be without it. It was his constant, and I knew how important constants were. I've always had difficulty empathising, and up until I was diagnosed I didn't even know the meaning of the word empathy, let alone that this sort of emotion existed at all, but I felt I could empathise perfectly with Mr Doughty. At the time I regarded it as being on the same wavelength, but with hindsight I can see with clear conviction that it was empathy.

Mrs Taylor endured a living nightmare as the Head of Year, yet surprisingly she had an astonishing supply of faith in her pupils. Like Mr Osbourne and Mr Doughty, she stood strong as a bold and true example of philanthropy. She was the one who encouraged me to share my problems, to come out of my shell and actually talk. They gave me a voice, and I gave them an earful - when you've been oppressed and bullied into submission for so long, a chance to talk means a chance to rant, and they never once complained. They accepted me for all that I was. Maybe because I didn't shout abuse at them like the other kids did, or play pranks on them such as locking them out of the classroom or stealing their bags (I've always hated being a goody goody by the way, but what chance did I have to be a rebel?). If it wasn't for Mr Osbourne I would have legged it out of school at break time, as fast as my treetrunk legs could carry me. If it wasn't for Mr Doughty I wouldn't have even registered at all. If it wasn't for Mrs Taylor my head would have spontaneously combusted.

In college I found more teachers who helped: Kevin Murphy and Faith Ressmeyer in English Literature; Faith Moody, Lesley Thomas, Jan Harker and Joel Tahoulin in Business Studies. These teachers all made so many concessions for me, and also provided a shoulder to cry on many a time. Initially I didn't see eye to eye with Kevin (I thought he hated me, so I was reluctant to do any work he set me, and sat in the class sulking most of the time while the other students all chatted to each other and produced excellent essays - it was also a mutual hate thing with me and them - Me versus Them is more appropriate), but eventually we managed to reach an understanding.

Faith Resmeyer in English Literature and the Business Studies department were fantastic. They made so much time for me, and really made me feel like a worthwhile cause. They became like this collective agony forum for me, and their counselling wasn't too bad either! Jan Harker s office became another one of my refuges, and both Faith Moody and Faith Resmeyer gave up valuable time for me when they should have been eating their dinner or drinking coffee. I honestly can't thank them enough.

With the right teachers, an Asperger student can flourish - I'm proof of that. OK, so I may not be the most intellectually-gifted person on the planet, or have that many qualifications, but I began school from below rock bottom. Those teachers provided a ladder for me to get through the manhole and to climb up into the average bracket - which by any definition is exceptionally good for someone with a disability. I sincerely hope I'm not the only Asperger student who was lucky like this - I really, really do.

Chapter 3
Obsession and Depression

Young obsessions

It is a well known fact among the autistic collective that a lot of people with Asperger's syndrome have obsessive personalities. I wouldn't go so far as to say every Asperger person is like this, but in my experience, I've only encountered one who doesn't fit this mould. These infatuations can be about anything - tangible objects such as trains, aeroplanes, trees and stamps; specific eras of fashion or genres of music; cult things - such as cult movies, cult TV programmes, cult novels, and possibly even religious cults; hobbies and careers; and finally people - primarily those of the far-fetched dream variety. I was no exception. My preferences began with plastic objects such as bottles, My Little Ponies (I collected 44 in total - lining them up along my windowsill in alphabetical order) and Barbies. I then progressed to people. Between the ages of 8 and 12 I obsessed about women who I admired and desperately wanted to emulate, whether fictitious or not. One particular character was Hewlett and Martin's Tank Girl - a feisty Australian comic book bitch-heroine who could kick the living daylights out of anyone who dared cross her path. She had a punk lad/kangaroo hybrid called Booga as a boyfriend, and a rowdy crew of friends consisting of men, women, other similar lad/kangaroos, a brilliantly hilarious fashion-conscious talking koala, Camp Koala, and an aardvark - Mr Precocious - among various others. I was totally infatuated with her because she was everything that I was not - tall, attractive, hard-talking, hard-hitting, tough, popular, independent and in demand. I read Hewlett and Martin's comic books religiously, until I could recite them word for word. I must have looked ridiculous, spouting Tank Girl phraseology mid-conversation, when it bore no relevance to anything. A typical example could be:

> Mum: What did you do at school today?
> Me: Who the hell is David Essex anyway Booga? And by the way, Camp Koala says you're batting first.

Adolescent obsessions

Tank Girl was my last ever female obsession. After her, I transferred my attention to men I fancied who, like all my previous obsessions, were entirely unobtainable. Robbie Williams, Blur's Damon Albarn, David Duchovny, Ewan McGregor, The Prodigy, a few superstar DJs - the list goes on. But in this instance my obsessions reached new heights. I was stubborn and wouldn't accept that these men were out of my reach, and consequently, I did something really stupid - I became a maniacal stalker.

Regrettably, at the time, I honestly didn't realise the severity of my actions, and I just want to apologise candidly for the trouble I've caused those people, and also apologise to myself for the humiliation I brought upon myself. Stalking is a serious offence, and I cannot ever reminisce on that ugly chapter of my life without shivering. I feel eminently guilty when I think of the ludicrous things I did just to get attention from the men I was infatuated with, and I don't think that guilt will ever be erased. OK, so I never threatened to do anyone harm, but what I did do certainly wasn't far off. I did stupid things, incredibly stupid things.

For instance, there was this one time I left 10 messages on this guy's answer phone, each message confessing my undying love for him and how I wanted him to leave his girlfriend for me and we'd elope to Gretna Green and get married. He never replied to me, so I just continued to bombard him with emails and love letters, assuming that if I proved how much I loved him, he would reciprocate. There I was, holding out for him, like Shakespeare's lovesick Juliet, and months passed before it dawned on me that waiting for a reply was tragically hopeless. Laugh all you like, but I was deadly serious at the time! I shudder just thinking about it. How could I have been so stupid?

Here is a rather corny love poem I wrote while totally obsessed with someone. I hope he never gets word of it, but then again how could he?

To The Man Who Will Never Know

I gazed at the stars
Up high in the sky,
And I created a story
In which you were mine.

And I'd write you the letter,
And I'd write you the book,
And I'd reach across the oceans
And force you to look.

In an ideal world
I'd be the one to set you free,
And I'd tear out my broken heart
For you to see.

Every moment I awoke
I clenched my teeth in prayer,
And I prayed that you'd know me,
Wished that you would care.

What kind of girl am I
To obsess over you like this
And let you rule my life?
What kind of girl am I
To prolong this emotion
When it hurts me like a knife?

And I wish I could stop wanting you
And I wish I could stop needing you,
Tell myself
"Forget it - it will never happen"
And stop bleeding for you.

Current obsessions

I am obsessed about my weight. I'm chubby, I'm robust, I'm big-boned, I'm wide-framed - and I'm obsessed. Yes, I love myself so much I'm infatuated with me! Narcissus' vanity was nothing compared to mine! When I look in the mirror I chant out loud "Mirror mirror on the wall, who is the fairest of them all?" And the mirror replies "Not you, you dozy cow. You are pure Hackett, so you are."

And the mirror is right, I hate my appearance. I hate it every time I try to squeeze into a size 14 and fail. I cringe every time I do the masochistic ritual of stepping on the scales, only to discover I've gained another two pounds. I want to burst into tears every time I catch my grotesque reflection in a shop window or a mirror. Jesus I hate mirrors! Every time I see one I feel this overwhelming impulse to just smash the damn thing into a billion pieces.

My confidence has been completely decimated because of my ugly form, which is why I can't get a boyfriend (not that I actually want one right now). Plenty of men prefer bigger women, so I know that if I put my mind to it I could have any man I wanted. But it's the self-esteem factor that fails me. You can't disguise insecurity and self-hatred through make-up or layers of clothing, because it always shows. I'm forward, friendly and could talk for Britain. I can be outgoing when I'm in the right mood, I can talk to anyone (or at least try). I'm confident rather than shy - but I'm not self-confident. I've pretended to be, but men have seen through it. So I've given up trying to pull, because if I did manage it whilst hiding behind my facade, the real me would soon emerge and the boyfriend would throw me in the bin again. At the end of the day, I can deduct that what a lot of men find most attractive in a woman is her self-esteem and confidence - and not her dress size. So if I could muster this self-esteem somehow, I'd be right in there!

I was reading a magazine article on being positive about your curves with avid interest, in hope of finding an original solution to boosting my self-confidence. However, all the solutions to beating that negative perception problem seem so ridiculous - too ridiculous to try. Actually, every solution I've ever read in any magazine seems downright stupid. I've tried standing in front of the mirror repeating "I am beautiful and worthwhile" 50 times, and all It's done for me is give me a sore throat. I've tried focusing on one aspect of my body and trying to admire it, but there's really nothing to admire about fingernails which have been chewed down to virtually nothing. I've tried looking at other girls and imagining they've got elephant's trunks for noses, but that's only brought me angry responses: "What are you looking at?"

Steel chains of jealousy bind me. I'm just so envious of Catherine Zeta Jones, Martine McCutcheon, Geri Halliwell, Carol Vorderman and co. losing all that weight. I honestly wish I could be happy for these once-chubby celebrities who achieve perfect size 6 or 8 figures, but instead all I feel is those old steel chains filled with livid green slime, again. Why? Because I can't lose weight like them, even if I tried. When you spend two hours every day religiously tugging on a rowing machine, abstain from virtually all the fatty, calorie-laden foods, and banish every excuse to be sedentary. My weight should be sinking, but the only thing that sinks around here is my self-confidence. I cannot speak for anyone else, but when my motivation and self-confidence reach rock-bottom, it significantly increases my capacity for jealousy and hatred. If I knew I could lose the weight it wouldn't be so bad, but because it appears that I can't, everything looks pointless and the whole world is on valium.

Wallowing in depression

So then depression takes hold of me, and I wallow in it for a few days, deliberately annoying anyone I can to make them hate me as much as I hate myself. I refuse to leave the house too. I realise exactly what I'm doing and why I'm doing it, but that's not to say I enjoy it. Maybe I do, in some twisted way - perhaps I'm a self-destructive mechanism and I actually want to be miserable? It's understandable why some people would revel in their misery - they could be psychological masochists, or desperate to die, or just avid self-haters. They might feel they deserve to suffer because of significant failures in their lives, or they might have done something they saw as wrong and are ridden with guilt about it.

But me? I don't know why I would want to hate myself. I've experienced so much hate already, which is partly my fault, but I don't like hating and I don't like being hated either. I'm far from perfect I know - I've been a complete idiot due to my naivete and I'm not the world's most intelligent person - but in my opinion this isn't a justified reason for self-condemnation.

> ***Painkillers anyone?***
> *The world has a beautiful face*
> *but an ugly interior.*
> *The fiction is fabulous,*
> *but reality is drearier.*
> *Outside is smooth, unblemished skin*
> *inside is a migraine*
> *- the pain it holds within.*

Comfort eating

A diary extract from 11th July 2000:

> Eating breakfast, dinner and tea all at one sitting - now that's a claim to fame! But not one that I'm exactly proud of. I don't reckon many other people - especially weight-conscious young women - could/would do that. The problem is I can't help myself. Like always, I've got no control over the situation. I'm always powerless. And it makes me want to die.

The problem is, just over a year back I was put on serious medication because of my health problems. I had lost around two stone after I left school, and was constantly elated at being able to fit comfortably into a size 10 every time. I was never skinny, but then again, the prospect of being another anorexic ferret clone didn't appeal to me. For the first time I was content in my body, even though I couldn't say the same about myself. The feeling of isolation, and the blatant flaws in my psychological structure, still tormented me, but at least I could look in the mirror and like what I saw in the physical sense. However, when I was put on medication, the pounds piled on, and on, and on. To add insult to injury, my appetite also increased, although I think this was probably a psychological thing and not the fault of the medication.

In my diary, I go on to say:

> What's worse is that I pile on the pounds where others lose them. It seems so easy for other young women who can gain 5lbs and lose them in just one week. But I can't

prove it, and I'm not so ignorant as to believe it really is the case for everyone else anyway. I appreciate that some women endure a constant battle with their weight - and one of those women is me.

I've got this love/hate relationship with food - love eating food, hate the weight I gain. Restaurants are torturous places when I scoff all three courses (the bigger the better - trust me, I get through mountains of food!). Worst thing is, I can't make decisions. I'm sitting there eating vegetable curry, yet my nose still twitches at the delicious scent of prawn korma, and then I'm wishing I could indulge in that too and hating myself in every sense. Sinful sinful sinful!

The problem, however, isn't with the eating - It's the exercise. Yes I love my food and would never dream of skipping a meal, but what it all boils down to is that when I'm exercising I feel great, I feel high, I feel confident and on top of the world. It's like a drug, and I want more. I know I'll end up paralysed in a wheelchair before I hit the menopause, but I can't help it - I love exercising. To look at me you'd think I'd never left the settee, but the need to exercise fuels my comfort eating. My psychological need turns into a physical one so I feel justified in doing five hours of exercise.
I've dislocated my knee and ankle once, and I'm sure my bones are rapidly wearing away, but that doesn't matter because as soon as I feel anything serious is about to happen, I'll end it all. Who wants to grow old and decrepit anyhow?

Where I found help

Janet M is a saint - well, as near to one as you can get! She has been instrumental in my life, and it was through her help that I was able to regulate my eating patterns. Once a nurse, she now works for the local mental health team, and is also an eating disorders specialist and nutritionist. With her expert knowledge of nutrition and psychological disorders (being an exact reverse of anorexia nervosa, overeating is a psychological disorder just as it is a physical one), Janet advised me on the right amount of calorific intake per day, how much exercise to do, and the sort of food to eat. Admittedly, at first I was in denial that I had a psychological disorder - I thought Asperger's syndrome was enough! I refused to take any advice from her. I shouldn't have been so obstinate, because in the end all it did was make me feel stupid.

However, Janet was persistent to make me see the error of my ways, and when I did she helped me to amend them. She told me to keep a food diary which she would check every week when we met at my house. I really appreciate her visits instead of me having to go into town to meet her because at the time my agoraphobia was very distressing.

In a matter of weeks, Janet had made the transition from adviser to social worker - and also friend. She seemed to sense that I didn't want to talk only about my problems, and often initiated conversations on other subjects. It was refreshing to be treated as a whole person, not just someone with an eating problem. I've visited many professionals in my life - both about my condition and my weight. Many looked upon me as if my syndrome or my weight problem was all that I was, making me feel like less of a person. I'm not sure if they meant to be like this, but it certainly seemed that way to me, and it really upset me - I've lost count how many times I walked out of a hospital or similar institution in floods of tears.

Now, over a year on, I'm managing to eat a reasonably sensible diet, and I hope I'll never top the scales at 12 stone again. It'll take a long time before I'm as slim as I used to be. A lot of my weight gain was due to the med, so I won't lose it until I'm off the bloody stuff. I'm just under 11 stone now and a size 18, which is certainly not perfect, but I suppose it's better than being a walrus. It's true that I've lapsed more times than I care to remember, but that's to be expected - sometimes being too good is bad. But I'm getting used to life without my everyday fish suppers, my McDonalds scoffathons and my ice-cream mountain challenges. It takes a lot of willpower and abstinence, but Janet is always there to keep me motivated.

The moral of this story is that other Asperger people don't have to suffer alone. A social worker can offer a tremendous amount of help and support and, like Janet, could turn out to be a good friend too. I would certainly advise fellow Asperger teenagers who, like myself, are having similar problems, to see someone from their local mental health team, or a social worker. I can't predict miracles - I can only speak for myself.

Why some Asperger people hate themselves

Some Asperger people use their negative experiences as a reason to be heavily critical of themselves, but I don't think they should do this because they are not entirely to blame. It is then that I reach the inevitable question of who is the claim for blame: is it solely one party or is it many? Many, I would expect. I don't think anything is due to only one factor, it is not entirely the Asperger person's fault, and neither is it entirely society's fault - it is a combination of both.

I also see it as a 'Catch 22' situation: the Asperger person is different and mainstreamers react to someone who differs from them - a few positively, but sadly, most negatively - which focuses the Asperger person on their differences compared to the majority of others. This can dent self-esteem, leaving them weak and vulnerable. This vulnerabilty to the comments of others could destroy any remaining self-esteem, resulting in further damage and maybe repeated patterns of abuse.

Asperger people aren't to blame for having Asperger's syndrome, and mainstreamers aren't to blame for reacting to what is different. It's only natural, after all. But are mainstreamers to blame for not tolerating the different person? In this instance I think blame is only involved where there is an element of choice. Toleration is a choice - you can choose when and when not to tolerate - and if the Asperger person is trying your patience you have the choice to ignore them (which isn't the answer to the problem, but it is still a choice nonetheless). Acceptance is a choice. Bullying and ostracising are choices. Having Asperger's syndrome is not a choice.

Can you relieve depression?

In an attempt to relieve my depression, I try to take a positive approach: I remind myself that I haven't always been this huge, and how I'll lose the weight within a few years; I try to accept myself as I am; I think of myself in comparison to larger girls; I tell myself that I have no less right than anyone else to enjoy life. Sometimes this manages to cheer me up, and sometimes it doesn't. And why can one approach have two different effects? Because, to be honest with you, I don't believe there is any singular approach to lightening or relieving an Asperger person's depression. As I have said before, there are many contributory factors to depression, so there are many depression-relieving approaches to explore, the majority of which are dependant on the situation, and whether you are trying to prevent depression or cure it.

A few possible ideas. You could try:

- Reminding the Asperger person that you care - offering comfort and support
- Paying extra attention
- Suggest seeing a counsellor or social worker
- Introducing a positive component - helping develop an interest or a hobby
- Arranging something special - a trip to a theme park, or maybe new clothes

It is likely you have already considered and/or tried these things, and received promising or disappointing results. No single approach is a complete solution - and maybe not even a combination of many - it all depends on the Asperger person. I am not trying to discourage you, but rather to clarify the fact that a failed solution is not your fault.

Personally, being comforted and supported during my periods of murky gloom helps, because I know that I am cared for despite my condition. If I didn't have my family and friends to comfort me, depression would have put me six feet under by now. Even if you don't relieve the Asperger person's depression, simply showing that you are there for them is essential. One Asperger friend, Haley, feels that her family don't understand her. She complains that they hardly ever pay her attention or show much interest in her because of her difference, which makes her feel irrelevant. She reflects other people's actions towards her onto herself - she feels no-one else likes her so she is encompassed in self-hatred. The only reason she is still here, she says, is because of her interests in animals and computers, which keep her occupied in times of boredom and strife.

Too much attention

On the other hand, showing the Asperger person too much attention might prove to be a bad thing. My mother took the whole attention thing too far and quizzed me about anything and everything, just to prove her interest in me, and this only annoyed me. Too much attention from my relatives also made me feel as if I was being interrogated - even though I knew this was not their intention. So be attentive to their needs rather than over-attentive, and be both proactive and reactive rather than just one of them. This is much easier said than done, however. Implementing a change in your approach to the Asperger person might take a while to do, and then there's another wait for results which can take some time.

Counselling

Seeing a counsellor is helpful to many people, although many Asperger people might not want to be counselled. Don't force counselling upon them - even if it is in their best interest - because it will only cause resentment. If, on the other hand, the Asperger person is content with being counselled, it is important to remember that not every counsellor is informed about the many facets of the Autistic spectrum, and is therefore unable to offer adequate help. It is much harder to communicate with an Asperger person than a mainstreamer, so the counsellor you choose has to be specialised in the Autistic field, otherwise there will be little or no understanding in the counsellor-client relationship, and consequently no improvement.

Gifts

The last solution I have offered is the most misused one of all. Some parents assume that material and monetary gifts can always provide happiness, but this is not true. The novelty of these treats is only temporary, and can only work for a certain period of time, before they become routine and boring. This is not to say they are ineffective though. They are effective, but only in the short-term, and are certainly worth using a few times in the hope of lightening the Asperger person's mood. However, they are only possible providing you have the resources - time and money.

Stick with it

Depression is a difficult subject to tackle, and there is no specific or easy way to cure it. It can be prevented for a short while only, because unless the significant factors contributing to it are removed, it will inevitably creep back.

So what can you do about it? I honestly don't know. The only advice I can offer is to listen to the Asperger person's problems and try to keep your patience, however difficult this may be. Give the person love and support, remind them that you will always be there, and in time the depression will hopefully subside. If they do not respond to affection then I would advise just allowing them their space - maybe they feel confined and need some time alone to clear their head? Just let them know you are trying to understand them - that won't solve the problem, but it should at least make them feel slightly better, safe in the knowledge that someone cares.

Chapter 4
Inferiority Complexes, Confusion
and Insecurity

Inferiority complexes: how come?

Inferiority complexes are common in Asperger people, and are most noticeable in two extreme forms of behaviour - bullying and withdrawal. Asperger people are not inherently nasty, but some find that bullying weaker people is a way to gain some control - for they have little control over the other elements in their lives. Bullying builds a sense of superiority. They may not realise there are other ways to improve their confidence. They might not know why they bully, or might not even realise they are bullying someone at all.

On the opposite side, the Asperger person could feel so inferior to everyone else that they are too frightened to express themselves, and are liable to be bullied.

Asperger people can develop inferiority complexes because of their lack of control over the world around them, or as a result of being bullied, failing at something, or not living up to their own or someone else's expectations. It is debatable, however, whether they are actually born with these feelings. Personally, I didn't see myself as inferior until I reached age eight. Then everyone else seemed to be excelling at everything and I just seemed to lag behind. As I grew older, the gap between me and other kids increased, and it was impossible for me to catch up. That is how my feelings of inferiority solidified.

My inferiority complex and how it confuses me

Diary extract from 16th July 2000:

An inferiority complex can affect every aspect of life. There are times when I feel inferior in everything that I am and do in comparison to others. I've studied how other people conduct themselves in reality and in films and TV, and always feel inferior. I know that these characters are based on ideals, and in fiction anyone can do anything, but they shroud my confidence nonetheless.

It is the 'true-to-life' and 'based-on-a-true-story' movies and TV programmes that really get to me. Feisty, tough-talking, take-no-shit-from-anyone women like Madonna and Erin Brokovich should inspire me, but instead they just depress me because I'm neither blessed with - nor have been able to learn - their wit, style, rapport or instant reflexes. These women won't take no for an answer and are never lost for words; they never stammer, stutter, make irrelevant comments or humiliate themselves. They never repeat themselves, are never incapable of enduring or winning an argument, and never totally bodge everything up. They specify their targets, aim, fire, and hit... bulls-eye. My shot, however, crashes to the ground as soon as it leaves my hand. I fail point blank.

And I'm crap at writing. I'm not trying to be a literary genius. I don't know many impressive words, and I certainly don't think I'm fluent at constructing intellectual sounding sentences. Some people seem to string them out like the alphabet, but no matter how hard I've tried to master this skill, I just can't. But hey, at least I'm being honest and not pretentious. Writing doesn't come naturally to me, unfortunately, but I make a genuine effort.

I keep reminding myself that basic, simple language does not mean I'm a bad writer, but yet again that little part of my brain that is perpetually critical of everything I do is screaming how imperative it is to have mastery over vocabulary - how much more impressive it is - how much more inclined people are to buy a book that is phrased intellectually.

But should I really care? This is where I confuse myself. To be honest with you, I don't care 50%. But what I really want is to not care 100%. This is **my** book, and if it's written badly and I receive major criticism then so be it. But I can't think like that - I'm not thick-skinned.

And I shouldn't care what others think of me as a person either, or should I? I want people to like me, so yes, I should care what they think of me so I can make myself more appealing. If I don't know what they think of me, how can I try to rectify my faults or make the most of my abilities? But shouldn't I just trust in myself anyway, regardless?

This here rant might sound defensive - like I'm hurling questions at you - but it's not. I'm not defending my right to care, because I can't even figure out if I should care or not. And anyway, I'm not confident enough to be defensive. I'm just confused and am trying to reach any sort of answer to these questions that rage in my head.

I think it's important to take how others see me into consideration, but not to the extent that I allow it to dictate my life. I think it's important to trust in myself and make my own judgements - to have independent thought. But sometimes I feel that I'm too stupid to trust in myself, and feel I need advice on every level.

There is so much more I want to say, but I just can't write it down. I'm not expert at converting my expressions into words, but then again, is anyone? Explaining how you feel and why is sure to be difficult for everyone to some degree. I know I am not alone in this situation, yet because of my inferiority complex I feel that I am.

More about confusion and uncertainty

This diary extract from 22nd July 2000 just about says it all:

> That seems to be the story of my life - I don't know. I'm unsure of everything and yet I'm sure that I'm sure of something. I'm indecisive but not indifferent. I'm a contradiction in terms. You've probably already noticed how I've contradicted myself several times.
>
> I'm confused about the world and its mainstream majority. What would it be like being mainstream? Would I even have these problems if I were a mainstreamer? Would I still be so confused? Is Asperger's syndrome as bad an affliction as I make out? And who am I anyway? Apart from being a representative of my syndrome, who am I, and most importantly, who will I become? Will I have status or will I just remain this feeble little doormat? I'm so incompetent I can't even decide on what I'm sure of and unsure of; what I know and don't know; what my opinions and judgements are, what views I hold; what my perception of the world is. I want to scream because I'm grotesque on the outside and incompetent on the inside.
>
> All this talk of being useless and pathetic shows how much of a pitiful weakling I am. No-one likes a self-pitying juvenile, let alone sympathises with one. But I want to tell them all: Stop, don't discard me. I need you to listen, even though it's very taxing on the patience. I'm not demanding your sympathy, and I'm not asking for your friendship. Just don't write me off as a hopeless case. But I won't plead any longer - it's for you to decide what you do. So if you think these depressive ramblings are all just a monotonous waste of words - or if my self-loathing irritates you - then you're under no obligation to stay. And to all the people who stayed for a while: thanks for at least trying to understand my condition (or were you just curious how the deranged mind of a manic depressive Asperger teenager works?), because you've done more than most people I've known - and I mean that candidly, in case you thought you detected rife sarcasm in that last sentence.

A philosophical question on insecurity

I'm not a psychologist, but I often ponder over the politics of the Asperger brain - why I do things the way I do and what these things mean. I want to translate myself psychologically so I can conduct further studies on myself and how my Asperger's syndrome affects me. Some Asperger people would object to being studied and then having their details shoved into a filing cabinet. I think studies on Asperger people are entirely necessary, because the more self-knowledge we have, the more opportunity we have to help ourselves. But I digress... So here's the question:

I wonder if you can psychologically assess what someone is like from what and how they write? If they use expressions such as "or something/nothing/anything/whatever", "do you agree?", "maybe", "I'm uncertain" and "does that mean..?" Are they insecure? Do they feel the need to seek reassurance from another source - or are these purely rhetorical questions? I know I'm a very insecure person, but strangely enough these phrases I use seem more of the rhetorical, in my opinion. I know my insecurity surfaces in my writing, yet I think I use my "maybe" and "or something" more as a habit. Hmmm, any takers on that one? And exactly how can you recognise insecurity? How is insecurity displayed in writing - through question marks, limited vocabulary, digression to some irrelevant subject, pedantic or abrupt sentences? Unless the writer actually states he/she is insecure, how is it possible to discern his/her insecurity? Am I myself way too insecure for pondering all these questions and is this easily recognisable in my words?

Questioning

What you can discern from the above rant is that I'm the questioning type of Asperger. Believe me, I question practically everything! Sometimes I think I'm too inquisitive for my own good - curiosity killed the cat, after all - so I've taught myself how to disguise it most of the time; although this wasn't the case when I was younger and I'd be constantly spouting questions to whoever was in earshot.

This was a contributing factor to my peers dislike of me, and now it's easy to see why. Before I was bullied into silence, a typical questioning spree of mine might be:

> *"Hey Lucy, how come your hair was blonde when you were a baby but is brown now? Do you dye it?"*
> *"Hey Emma, how come you're wearing a pink hair-bobble today when you were wearing a blue one yesterday?"*
> *"Hey anyone, why isthere a daisy right there and not one over there?"*
> *"Hey Mr Wallis, how come this pen is shaped like this and that pen is shaped like that?"*
> *"Hey Mrs Ashford, how come there's a rip in your tights?"*
> *"Hey James, how come your Dad never picks you up from school any more?"*
> *"Hey Louise, when is your goldfish going to be big enough to eat?"*
> *"Hey Simon, what does your baby sister's vomit look like?"*

Not exactly hard to see how my inquisitive nature often got me into trouble! Why did I ask these obscure questions? Well, basically because I didn't have a scooby doo (clue) how to hold a conversation, so I assumed a sea of questions would suffice instead. I didn't see anything wrong with this because I didn't understand how unusual my behaviour was.

How to advise the extra inquisitive Asperger child

Don't repress - advise. If you tell the child to quit questioning altogether then he/she will probably only rebel or become subdued. Advise the child when it is and when it isn't appropriate to ask questions. Direct them on the questions that are OK to ask and the ones that are not. Maybe make up little picture tests for them, or make up a short play about questions with them.

Another useful way to help inquisitive Asperger children is by providing a children's encyclopaedia, which you could explore together, or they could read by themselves - that certainly helped me.

Chapter 5
Emotions

Paranoia

Where emotion is concerned, there are various categories of Asperger people, but I will concentrate on explaining the most obvious two. I hate to categorise and generalise, but in this case it's necessary. There's one type who have an oblivious outlook on things, and would remain unaffected even if World War 3 began on their doorstep - and there's another type who are so overly sensitive it's ridiculous. I see myself as the latter.

I was sensitive to change. I was terrified of it, because change leapt into the unknown, and I couldn't get my head around the concept of exactly what the unknown was. I was so sensitive to the ever-changing world around me, and everything I did at school was dictated by others, so I had no control. To compensate I had to exert my control by building a definite routine out of school life.

I had immense difficulty keeping my composure when in a new situation - like mum cooking tea five minutes later - in a different environment, like visiting someone's else's house. I needed everything to be in the same place. I wanted stability, I demanded routine and monotony, and I literally went to pieces if any aspect of my out of school life was altered. I felt that everything was controlling me and everyone was oppressing me.

This drove me to become severely paranoid about anything and everything, whether it appeared to be relevant or not - an ornament out of place, a dripping tap, an untidy desk, a look, a glance, a distant laugh, a cough or sneeze, a car horn, a fire alarm, the sound of breaking glass. However irrelevant these factors seemed to the majority of people, you wouldn't believe how personal they felt to me, or how easily I managed to relate them to me. Take a laugh, for example: regardless of how far away it was, I was convinced it was directed maliciously at me. If someone coughed I interpreted it as a hint that they thought I was germ-ridden. If a mug or saucer had been moved, I believed someone had done it to frighten me. I was terrified of everything.

Augmented sensory perception

Due to the extent of my over-sensitivity, I often felt I had a sort of augmented sensory awareness. This happened, however, only when all was quiet and still, so I cannot really prove that my senses were heightened at all - although I would like to believe that they were (and still are), rather than pointing the finger at my over-active imagination.

Sometimes, I believed I saw and felt visions too. Once, I was standing at the bus stop, and from the deep dark depths beneath my jittering feet, something ominously stirred, something rumbled. Three days later, parts of Japan were devastated by one of the worst earthquakes ever.

Andrew Miles (originally a co-writer of this book, who couldn't maintain it because of the time needed for his studies) has experienced similar things, and devised a theory to explain them, which he called the Gaian Theory. What Asperger people lack in social intuition is compensated for in their enhanced sensory intuition. Kristi Jorde offers a similar sort of experience in her book *A Child Of Eternity* (1995, Piatkus, London). Jorde reveals how, using a breakthrough technique called Facilitated Communication, her Autistic daughter Adriana brought across an extraordinary message from the world beyond, which could be explained by Andrew's Gaian Theory. Studies are needed to establish the validity of acute sensory intuition in Asperger/autistic people.

Because of these dynamic sensory surges I was often prone to stress, and this was generally an extremely heavy bout of stress. I found I could get stressed out - and unnerved to the point where I was screaming like a lunatic - by practically anything. (Not as many things have this affect now I am older and more knowledgeable.)

Here is a true event recorded in early August, explaining just this:

It is a hot summer day. I am sitting on the settee, reading a magazine, when suddenly, I notice a bizarre buzzing sound - so loud I feel it vibrating in my bones - emanating from the kitchen, even though the kitchen door is closed. *Brrrrzzzzzzzzzzzzzzz.*
It's a bumble bee! I panic, sitting bolt upright (why can't I ever correct my posture in situations where it's necessary?) Then, I listen again, carefully. *Baaarrrrrzzzzzzzzzz.*
No, it certainly wasn't a bumble bee. No way could a bumble bee make such a distinctive, electric-razor type buzz. But I'm sure I can hear the slow drone of a deep hum.
Buuuuuuaaaaarrrrrrrzzzzzzzz.
 "Oh God no," I silently plead, "don't let it be a hornet. Please don't let it be a hornet."

I crook my head round the wall and try to peek through the window in the door, in the hope of confirming my worst suspicions. It didn't work. I return my head to its previous position and monitor my own desperate heartbeat, inwardly repeating "not a hornet, not a hornet, please not a hornet"continuously.

 1...2...3...4...5 seconds. Baboombaboombaboom! My heart thuds. Another five seconds. Baboombaboombaboom! Neither my heart beat nor that awful buzzing subsides. Where is my logicality when I need it? Where is my rationality? How come I can never maintain a calm composure when it would be useful?

There is a sudden tapping at the window. I gasp and swing my head round, then breathe a sigh of relief when I find the culprit to be a twig.

"I'm going mad," I think, panic immediately setting in, "I'm going pure mental. That twig sounded more like a stone - how can such a small thing make such a loud noise? And it's outside, so how can I hear it as though it's only an inch away? Maybe I'm seeing things. Maybe it's all in my mind. And is that a hornet in the kitchen or am I imagining that too? Yes, I'm definitely going mad."

But another part of me wants to protest against this deduction. "I'm not going mad!" It screams at me, "My hearing's gone haywire and I can't figure out why, but I am NOT going mad!"

Then, my eardrums are stung with that frightful buzzing again, and I shudder. Two voices are waging a war in my head:

"It's the washing machine," says the first.

"It's a hornet," says the second.

"Washing machine."

"Hornet."

"Naw, it's gotta be the washing machine."

"A washing machine doesn't hum like that. It's a hornet for sure."

The buzzing transpired to be the dreaded hornet after all, by the way, but I still cannot emphasise enough how important my augmented sensory perception is to me, so I'll continue with another exert from my diary - this one from early July whilst staying with relatives in America:

 I'm frightened, sitting here at the kitchen counter at 2:31am. I can hear creekings and soft, meticulous shufflings from the room opposite - sounds resembling footsteps, muffled thuds, and the continual whirr of the air conditioning. I'm all alone down here, but I can't help feeling that tinge of anxiety tugging at my mind. This fear is totally irrational, I know, because there's no-one down here except me. These noises could be from upstairs or from the basement. I feel stupid for being afraid.

...... BIG THUD.

Now I'm certain that wasn't from upstairs - it was right behind me. For crying out loud I should not be frightened, but I am, and continue to be.

Is that whispering, or is it just my imagination playing tricks on me? Scrapings on the ceiling - someone's moving furniture around up there...Relentless creaking, humming and breathing?

OK. I'm terrified! There, I've admitted it, now who/whatever you are please give me peace and stop distracting me from writing this oh-so-important-would-be-highly-acclaimed piece of literature? Go on! Bloody well get lost why don't you?! You do not control my emotions - I do! I won't permit myself to fear you.

Well, whether you can hear my gesture of defiance or not, I will not surrender to the fear you are trying to impose upon me.

What is fear?

But what is fear anyway? Is it intuition or rationality - actually some disguised form of benevolent force, here to save us from danger or from ourselves, here to guide us and to differentiate between what's right and wrong? Is fear strength or cowardice? If we resist our fear, are we strong, and if we surrender to it are we cowards? Or does it give us courage by forcing us to confront the reality of our fears and try to address them in a rational manner?

I know every intelligent life-form is predisposed to fear, so it is obviously necessary to our survival and is not a personal failure. If mice weren't instinctively afraid of cats then they wouldn't run from them; if humans weren't afraid of animals stronger and more dangerous than ourselves, then lions and tigers would be allowed to roam freely around zoos, mauling and eating as they saw fit. I don't think that arachnophobia would exist if there were no poisonous spiders or scorpions. Common phobias concerning arachnids, snakes, heights, water, open and closed spaces, are manifestations of our fear of death - obviously - although agoraphobia and claustrophobia (agoraphobia especially) are to a lesser extent. I believe they concern themselves more with a fear of helplessness, loss of control, oppression and confinement, rather than death - but still, they are nonetheless perfectly rational phobias.

So are my fears irrational? When you're alone somewhere, surrounded by darkness and obscure noises, your mind can play tricks on you, and fear develops from this and breeds more fear - and before you know it you've convinced yourself there's something to be afraid of. I think this applies to everyone, Autistic or not, but I also think it's the overly-sensitive Asperger people who feel it the most.

Conflicting noises

When I was younger I was terrified by the conflicting hustle and noise in crowded places such as supermarkets and towns, because the sensory overload was all too much for me to comprehend. So many sounds, so many smells, so many things to see, so many different textures (taste wasn't relevant in this case)...These things confused me so much, and I was unable to concentrate on them all simultaneously - it was daunting for me.

I must have looked a real idiot bursting into tears and yelling at the top of my lungs when placed in a crowded situation, but I didn't even acknowledge my terrified outbursts were at all strange until I was seven. Before this realisation, whenever the torrent of noise and movement became too much, I'd run as far away as I could get (usually one of the far corners of the playground, a toilet cubicle, or a park bench - depending where I was at the time), cover my ears and crouch on the ground in a tight little ball, often rocking backwards and forwards and side to side.

As with noise, quietness is oppressive, disconcerting - sometimes even frightening.

Loneliness

An extract from my diary, dated 18th October 2000:

It's 1:09 am and I'm feeling upset. For a start, my special medicated facewash, my moisturiser, my toothbrush and various other items have gone missing and I can't find them anywhere. I know they are here but their current absence bothers me all the same.

I am also upset about my compulsive overeating and constant weight gain. Every time I look in that dreaded mirror my reflection is fatter, spottier and uglier than before. But you've already heard all that...

And of course there's always the reminder that I haven't slept for almost 48 hours, but I'm not entirely sure if that has much relevance, because I experience this same feeling on normal nights too.

But there's something else - something I can't quite put my finger on right now. It's a feeling akin to severe loneliness (and I know loneliness plays a significant part in it), combined with a deep-rooted self-hatred and a fear of stillness. Because the house is entirely still, apart from me moving around and the babble of the TV. I'm not frightened of being the only one awake, I'm simply fearful of a noiseless, inert atmosphere - but I don't know why. I know I'm not liable to be attacked. It's unlikely the roof will collapse on me. This house has never been haunted before. So I should be able to work out why the silence scares me. But I can't.

I think it's not so much the silence as the loneliness that causes the problem. I feel so alone most of the time and the feeling is exacerbated late at night when my parents have gone to bed, it's too late to call my friend; there's no decent TV or movies to watch so I can't use the TV as substitute company; and there's absolutely nothing to occupy me except to go to bed and try to sleep. It's just a plain, blank, drowsy nothingness - a feeling so present that it's actually an all-pervading (and all-encompassing) entity in itself. It's very existence seems to dampen everything around me. Everything is dull and lifeless and still - and this concept kind of frightens me.

Safety and security are not issues here - I feel perfectly safe and secure (secure in the sense that I know the house won't be broken into - not emotionally) as I am. I recall a line from an ATB song: "It's the loneliness that's the killer". And it's so true.

I am strangely desperate, but about what I don't know. Desperate for something to do to keep me from sleeping (even though, after almost 48 hours awake, I'm extremely fatigued). Desperate for something miraculous to happen and brighten up this drab existence. When I was a kid I used to think that staring into space and concentrating exclusively on a specific wish would make that wish happen. I used to believe that it was possible to make dreams come true right before your very eyes. Right now I want to see translucent bubbles float out of the walls; I want a friend to phone; I want to see UFOs flash across the midnight sky; I want to know that very soon I'll be back to eight-and-a-half stone and my skin won't get ruined any further and my debilitating bodily problems will cease...

But every wish and dream seems too distant now. Whilst in this pessimistic state of mind, nothing can ever be good. So I have to quit the pessimism. Somehow.

Boredom and philosophy

Like many Asperger individuals, I've got a short attention span. This means that I get bored too quickly, and when I get bored I inevitably complain - providing there's someone to complain to. If, however, I'm alone and bored, then my mind jumps to other places and my philosophical streak resurfaces. This has proved to be the case for other Asperger people too - my good friends Andrew and Trish agree. My point here is that there is a common theory that Asperger people have trouble embracing so-called abstract concepts. Call me a peasant, but I really don't understand what abstract concepts are supposed to be. Exactly

how do you define something as abstract? Is the following rant an abstract concept?:
"Have you ever experienced the feeling that everything ultimately amounts to nothing - that everything is nothing? It's a weird and frightfully disconcerting concept. Feeling everything - even the most spectacular of events, holidays and parties - to be too limited. There's got to be something greater and more wonderful, somehow..."

I've studied philosophy, liked it and understood it - it's only the massive amount of pedantic phraseology that makes it difficult. This, some say, is exactly what philosophy is all about - long-winded sentences, pedantic explanations. I agree that expressing oneself in the most articulate of terms is the method favoured by many a philosopher, but I don't agree that this is the core of the subject. The concept is the framework - the foundation - which words and phrases are built upon; so can't it be true that it is the concept the words express, and not the words themselves, that defines philosophy? The concept is the skeleton, and without that, the meat - the words - would have nothing to cling to. If the concept is there, is the literary style really all that important? Perhaps that's what the abstract concepts theory means - how much the concept and the words expressing it relate to each other, which one is most dependent? It's one of these cliched chicken and egg scenarios again isn't it - which one was first? Well, you need words to think of a concept, but you need to imagine a concept before you commit it to words...I don't know, I could be here forever!

Anyway, enough of my rambling. I'll let you deduce whether I can understand abstract concepts or not. Maybe if I had an exact definition of what they were, then I could tell you.

Disorientation

A diary extract from 21st July 2000:

> I think this is what is commonly known as disorientation; even home doesn't feel like home - nowhere does. The world is huge and the universe is infinite, yet I cannot think of any place where I could be inconspicuous - where I wouldn't stick out like a sore thumb - I am unable to settle in any one place, because nowhere is right. I can't actually verify this, because I haven't been to every place on earth, so this feeling is stupid and irrational. Isn't there always somewhere?
>
> Probably. If you're a social misfit in one place you're not necessarily the same in another - it depends on the society and it's values and culture, expectations, attitudes. We are all individuals in our own right, but society falls into a number of different, broadly-defined groups or categories - for example the aspirers, the dreamers, the realists, the cynics, the achievers, the conformists and the rebels, the fashion-

conscious, the popular, the eccentric, the conservative, the liberal, the superficial and shallow - and within these groups there will emerge a variation of subgroups. Some are cliquey, some are not. Some are open-minded, some are not. Some are self-assured, some are not. Some are proud, some are not. Some are this and others are that, some are ying and others yang etc. Therefore, hypothetically, there has to be at least one group where Asperger people would not be judged, criticised or harassed. Not everyone is a bully or an oppressor. I'm positive of that.

Yet I'm still disorientated. I can't put my finger on exactly why I feel this way right now - or even if this feeling is disorientation. It's as if I'm enclosed within a very dark room, surrounded by shapes that I can't touch but can almost make out. Almost. In my mind I reach for them, I try to connect my hands with them so their mystery can be solved, and I am practically there, but that one further inch can never be surmounted. So near and yet so far.

This feeling disturbs me. I wouldn't say I hate it or fear it, though. It causes me to lose my way; it distracts me; it's tenacious and it won't relinquish its firm grip on me; yet I believe it is actually trying to enlighten me - trying to tell me something about myself and my condition.

So therefore it is more of an obstacle to climb over. It might be blocking my view right now, but it only does so to make me summon the strength to conquer it. It might take a while, but ultimately all the sweat and blood and tears will be worth it. My Asperger's syndrome will not be an impediment forever - one day it will be a gift.

Finding Reality

Morning always comes too soon
Because the night
Always
Goes
Too
Quickly,
I can't escape from anything
Even if I wanted to.
Lying in bed wasting the day away
I don't feel fit to socialise
Not
Fit
To
Socialise.

Give me pills
Give me drink,
Anything that I can think
Of,
Just
To
Stay
Alive.
In my mind I can see clearly
But
Outside my vision is blurred
And I don't want to see anything
Or anyone...

If I had an inspiration
Would my life be so confusing,
Would I even have to compare?
Turn away
See if I care.
If I felt no fear, no trepidation
Would the world be more amusing,
Would I have the strength to dare?
I'll answer my own questions
Find my reality outside,
One day,
Out there.

Chapter 6
Not For The Faint Hearted

Rain and Traffic

It's raining -
Icy particles shattering all around.
There's a two mile tailback -
Tyres bruising the concrete ground.

Sports cars -
Those streamlined creatures that grace the road.
My mum's Metro -
Sluggish and battered like a metal toad.

Ominous clouds -
Stealthily moving in across the bleeding sky.
The whole world's in a comedown -
Even the tankers have their own reason to sigh.
As if nothing and no-one
Has ever known what love is.

And the rain is not cleansing.
And the fire is not soothing.
And the breeze is not liberating.
And the traffic is not moving.

Self-pity

An excerpt from my diary, from 23rd March 2000:

This is a no win situation. I feel pathetic so I pity myself. I say I'm pathetic, they say I'm not (liars and cowards that they are), I insist I am, then they say I'm pathetic for saying that! I can't even say I'm snivelling and wretched to myself without reproaching myself for it, then in turn reproaching myself for trying to dismiss my contemptible state, because all I am is weak, pitiful and pathetic. It's a vicious circle I have to escape from, if I only knew how.

Security - that's all I want: to know they do honestly like me and care about me. I ask them to tell me they like me - even though I know it annoys them - because I'm never satisfied. Because I'm insecure. I need constant reassurance that I'm liked, and they dislike me for this, because they can see my insecurity and paranoia and are unable, unequipped to deal with it.

I don't blame them - it's entirely my fault. I have to convince myself that reassurance really isn't necessary - because it's not. I don't need it and I don't want it - yet I do, and I'm plagued with this nagging thought in my head, instructing me to ask them again and make them tell me they appreciate me.

And I have a lot more problems than most people, and probably a whole host more to come. Osteoarthritis? Some sort of cancer? Thicker depression? Even more excessive weight gain - confinement to existence in a wheelchair because I'm too fat to walk? Please God. Please don't inflict any more troubles upon me. Please, if you're listening, I'm begging you, I can't stand it. I've already taken various methods of suicide into consideration. There's no outlet for the frustration I feel inside. I want to smash everything in the house. I want to slit my wrists. I want to put a bullet in my useless brain. I could number the reasons why:

1) All my friends have jobs, whereas I'm too incompetent to be employed by anyone. I'm dyspraxic, I stammer, and I'm perpetually having to get instructions reaffirmed, as I'm too dense to understand first, second or even third time.

2) My favourite CD is broken and I can't afford to buy a new one. Why does every valuable material possession of mine get ruined or damaged? It seems that I have this incredible power to destroy or injure anything I value. Maybe I'm too worthless to deserve anything? My life is always dented in some way.

3) Whoever said "no matter how big the amount of negativity in life, one can always find room for positivity," was talking a load of bull. There's nothing positive in my life, so how am I supposed to find any positivity? You tell me how, Mr Whateveryournamewas! Just tell me how, and I'll scrape the grit out your fingernails for the rest of your life! And just for the sake of pitying myself even more I'll churn out yet another reason to hate myself.

4) I'll see all my friends getting married or living with partners, probably having kids, and if life continues to be as shite for me as it is right now, then I can't envisage myself having any of that. It's not the kids part I care about - it's the relationships and sex. All my friends will be getting it, and I won't. No man will ever desire or love a fat ugly goblin like me. I'll grow old alone... That's if I live to be old, which right now doesn't look very likely. Plus I haven't accomplished any of my goals. Always the underachiever.

Self mutilation

Now I have reached this very difficult and disturbing section of my story. This won't be to everyone's liking, but as this is an honest and open account of my experiences as an Asperger youth, I think that it is important for you to know about it.

Many other Asperger youths that I am in contact with harm themselves and some are even suicidal. They have told me that they harm themselves because their life is depressing and they want to suffer - which is exactly the same as me. Depression is a horrendous thing. During these bouts of severity I am consumed with paranoia, anger, hatred and no confidence. I feel that I am a feeble, weak and incompetent failure. When I'm down I can't defend myself verbally, I can't apply myself properly in any argumentative situation. I wish I could be a bitch instead, at least then I could fight my corner. Another thing about depression is that anything can cause a tear: a tune, chord sequence, a picture, an object out of place, a speck of dust on a picture frame... and then all I can think about is how to escape the pain in my head, of which the only route is through the physical. Self-abuse can take many forms. It's not all about razors and knives as my account will show you.

I've tried to relieve it, but never seem to be able to. I try dancing to my favourite music or jogging round the house with a walkman on, but I always turn out exercising to the extremes - until I've got blisters on my feet, pulled muscles, fractured wrists/ankles, bruises, cuts - because I feel I need to punish myself.

Most of the time I exercise moderately and it does relieve any pent-up stress. It's just when depression has got its mind-forged manacles clasped around me that all good in me becomes bane. I try doing things that should cheer me up, yet the part of me that thrives on self-hatred and pain twists the situation to its' advantage and I find myself jogging for three hours with shoes two sizes too small on just to kill my feet, thinking how I deserve to suffer. Then my hatred escalates and I crave to hurt more, if only to forget for a few small moments everything else in my life and just to concentrate on the physical pain that's here and now. This is why my hands and arms are tattooed with scars.

Upsetting

The myth that self-mutilation is an attention-seeking device is purely that - a myth. In fact, self-mutilation is a very personal and private affair. Many people assume that this is for selfish reasons. In fact, it is due to embarrassment or consideration for others or, sometimes, just because. It is not always true that Asperger people are self-centred and uncaring. A number of my Asperger friends say they keep their self-mutilation secret because they don't want to upset their families.

Lagging behind when everyone else is moving ahead

I have found that everything seems to have a delayed reaction. Maybe this is my Asperger's syndrome or maybe it is just me, but whatever the reason, sometimes it really upsets me. It seems as though all my friends are advancing to bigger and better places whereas I am trailing behind at a sluggish pace, missing out on everything. I realise this isn't actually the case, that it's just a depression-induced perception. I am using my time constructively, but in a different way to my friends. Where my friends work or study, I write books.

Not everything is a negative to me. I can, of course, appreciate how my negativity can be difficult to read about but I feel that it is important for me to tell all sides of my story. The positive and the negative.

One way I see myself is dragging my cumbersome bulk along while my friends sprint forward in romantic relationships. The majority of my friends will probably marry and have children, but somehow I don't think I will. Being in a sexual relationship right now isn't of utmost importance. I can envisage myself growing old with no partner, remaining a spinster to my dying day. It's as though my friends have all caught the express train to Lurve Central, whereas I have to settle for a bicycle (oh well, at least I'll get some exercise).

Waiting

She stands on the edge of the platform
Awaiting the train that's a half hour delayed.
She gazes silently ahead
Again.
The half hour shuffles reluctantly by
But no train appears
Maybe it's due to the repairs
A few miles up the track
Again.
An announcement blares out overhead
Another ten minutes till the train is expected
She watches as the perfect blue is extracted
From the sky, and stolen away
Again.
She paces up and down
Waiting for the wind to change
Silently cursing at the stranger
A hundred meters away

The woman whose arm is linked with her man
Again.
Ten minutes extend to twelve, then fifteen
She tries to find some interest
In the shapes that stand in contrast
To the eternity of straight lines
But the shapes are familiar and boring
And she's seen them all too many times before
And she knows she will see them
Again.
And she waits
Wondering what went wrong
And how much longer
She'll be waiting
For a train that's delayed
Again.

The difference between jealousy and an empathy bypass

I feel I am also trudging along in the 'sharing other people's happiness' lane. Now I honestly try to be happy for my friends when things go terrifically well for them, but I can't deceive myself - I have a problem with jealousy. You might think that me being unable to associate with my friends happiness is due to my apparent lack of empathy but it isn't. Empathy isn't instinctively embedded in Asperger people, which is why I've had to learn it over the years. I am easily prone to jealousy. More so, it appears, than mainstreamers. In my estimation, I feel this emotion more powerfully because of my condition - the same way I feel anxiety, paranoia and infatuation more powerfully.

Unable to maintain a steady job

When it comes to working, Asperger people aren't always the best of employees. I've only had three jobs in my whole life and have been sacked from all of them. One of the reasons for this is my poor co-ordination and motor clumsiness (Tony Atwood, *Asperger's Syndrome*, 1998, Jessica Kingsley Publishers Ltd., London) which is explained in detail in another section of the book. I am extremely clumsy, so you can imagine what happened during the two times I worked as waitress!

But it wasn't only motor clumsiness that lost me my first waitressing job, it was also my magnified sensitive streak - the part of me which made me cry at every insult thrown at me and every apparently nasty stare in the street. It was when a group of slim, attractive girls jeered at my size; when I burst out in tears because of how jealous I was of them and how much I loathed myself; when I was too clouded with rage and self-hatred to think straight and consequently walked slap-bang into a table, tripped over and fell flat on my face; when I hung my head in shame and stood there, letting everyone ridicule me; when I realised I couldn't take any more and ran out, bawling my eyes out.

I hope that short anecdote provided you with further insight into this sensitive streak of mine, how I am lost when it comes to dealing with my tormentors and how easily prone I am to anger and jealousy. Consider what you would have done in my situation, then compare it to what I did and you will see how Asperger's syndrome affects me.

But I ask you this, neurotypicals, what should I have done? With hindsight I realise that it would have been best to totally disregard the group of girls and battled with my over-sensitivity. I should have taught myself how to accept my size and how to keep a professional air about me, despite being jeered at. I should have stepped back from myself and reassessed the situation. Large girls like me are perennially taunted for the same reason - it's unavoidable - yet they strive to go on.

Was it my Asperger's syndrome that prevented me from amending myself? I think it was. Asperger's syndrome subdues my ability to think straight and rationally, to keep calm and collected even in the most trivial circumstances. I'm not trying to blame what could be a character flaw on my condition, but the fact that a significant number of my Asperger friends claim to experience a similar reduced capacity for calm and rational thought in the face of adversity. I associate this flaw with my condition. For me, this is conclusive evidence.

Chapter 7
Me Versus the Rest of Society

The Internal thoughts of Winston Smith in the Ministry of Love, 1984

No windows. No windows.
No portal to the outside world.
Even the light is contrived.
No natural anything.
Fabrication everything, everywhere.
They say we live in the Light.

Is it just a convenience
Or something more - a protection perhaps?
Or does a more sinister truth lurk behind it -
A truth so proficiently concealed,
Carefully lodged between the cracks in the atmosphere?
They say there is no such thing as Truth.

If a protection, then why and what for?
Who and what do I need
To be protected from?
Or is this their twisted form of protection against me?
Are they afraid?
They say they do this for our own Protection.

Was this place - this artifice,
Constructed by those in authority
To avoid blame?
To avoid responsibility?
This is their stability -
Their mask of woven lies to hide behind.

Whilst I am here,
Trapped like a rat in a cage,
I sometimes think I am unable to differentiate
Between fact and fiction, lies and truth.
But that's a lie.
And they know that.

Mirrors.

I think of it like this: society is one big mirror, consisting of billions of individual mirrors, one carried by each individual, the majority of which reflect each other. Asperger people, however, have frosted mirrors, so the reflections they receive are clouded and undefined. Some mirrors eventually clear, gaining the Asperger person a legible, possibly even nearly mainstream, understanding of reality. Some verge on the slightly blurred, some make it to the halfway sign, others fall marginally below, and others never change.

Scatty, logical, illogical - my Asperger brain!

My brain pattern (I'm sure there's a technical term here but I don't know what it is) changes depending on my mood. I am never just scatty for a whole day or just logical or illogical, but always a mixture of the three. There are some Asperger people who follow just one brain pattern all the time and others who don't.

What evil lurks in the mind of Nita Nutcase on a typical day in her college life?

10.13 am: I lazily survey the rows of magazines. Someone has scribbled "I am a bender" on Tony Blair's face, which causes me to think of my friend Fiona up in Stirling. Fiona, a prime example of an anti-establishment partisan. Fiona, who is so strong yet so insecure. I think everyone is insecure, no-one is perfect after all. Fiona, who's studying politics. I wonder how she's doing...

I am faced with a row of garish headlines: Guns Blazing, Explosives, Riot Police, Hunting Aliens, The Ultimate Guide to Keeping Horses, Bolshoi Ballet, 100% Digital etc. etc. blah de blah de bleuuuurgh. Does anyone ever actually read these magazines?

Students carrying a skeleton mould on the cover of *Parklife* magazine, with a banner reading 'National March For Education: Scrap Tuition Fees', raised high above the swarming throng of protesters. Interesting... maybe if I've got more time I'll read the magazine because, to say the least, I am curious... Maybe it'll give me some inspiration?

I can hear that familiar taunting noise again. The one I've grown so accustomed to over the years. Sneering, laughing, mocking, all directed at me and my social failure. Of course, I knew this wasn't entirely true, it was only my paranoia nagging at me. At the back of the library someone is humming an *Annie* tune. How much do I hate musicals?! Infinitely.

I take a seat at an empty table and pull out my English assignment from the stuffy contents of my bag (I'm surprised some weird sort of life-form hasn't evolved in there yet, seeing as my bag is the perfect habitat). I open one of the designated poetry books and begin making notes. The poem I'm analysing right now is called *Caul*, which reminds me of the name Paul, then the dog *Old Saul* in Iain Bank's masterpiece *The Wasp Factory*, which is my favourite book to date. I love it to death, so much so that I'm going to read it again.

I work through *Caul, Away And See* then get distracted by a mathematical equation and subsequently lose the ability to spell. Many Asperger people can't do two things at once and I am no exception. If I try to solve an equation, I am unable to spell things correctly and vice versa. Concentrating on one thing is difficult enough. I skim through *Poet For Our Times*, then decide to catch a breath of fresh air out in the town. As I exit the library I pass a collective of nerds and feel their eyes burning into my back as I go by. "Ha, you'll never know that soon, this short dumpling of a girl will have more power and authority in her little finger than you'll ever have in your whole life," I laugh to myself inwardly and go off to hunt aliens.

I open the double doors to the outside world and am pushed into the wall by an unexpected influx of students, none of whom I make eye contact with. Bastards. Bitches. Tarts. Tools. I hate you all, grrrrrr! One of them is someone from my form, Laura, and she's not looking happy. Oh dear, poor her... Maybe she's broken a finger nail or gained a zillionth of a pound on her bum? Cow that she is. (I'm only jealous, I suppose.) Laura is best friends with a girl called Claire Mevins, who has recently become pregnant. So many girls my age have children now, it's like an epidemic. To be honest with you, I can't ever envisage myself having children - firstly I wouldn't want to risk passing Asperger's syndrome onto them, secondly because I am basically lazy, and any children of mine would most probably die of neglect.

It's baking hot outside but I keep my puffer jacket on. If I sweat rivers or die of dehydration I don't care - this jacket is staying on! Why? Because I hate my huge bulk of a body. The more I can cover it up, the better.

Despite the heat, the sky is overcast. Soon, Colchester can expect to be afflicted with a severe bout of pelting rain and I'm gonna be caught in it. (Nita, always the pessimist. It's sad I know, but please don't pity me.)

I am dragged out of my pit of negativity by a sudden thought: Many people will naturally assume that because Asperger people are Autistic, they will have an imagination bypass, won't be at all curious and won't consider the world around them. This is true in some cases, but in others it is false. I have always been what I call a random muser - what I mean by this is that I survey everything around me and try to extrapolate coherent meaning from it. I have a naturally curious nature and there are so many things I don't understand. I don't know how or why but something tells me these random musings of mine will be of some benefit to me one day. I just have this weird notion...Anyway, keep close attention. *Random Musings Of An Asperger Adolescent* might be on the shelves in the not-so-far future. And for those of you who just can't wait, here's an excerpt:

Random Musings on a Monday

1) Girl with pink hair, smoking a cigarette. If she doesn't get ridiculed, why do I?

2) Builders walking up and down the street. They were doing that when I arrived at college this morning. Do they actually do any work or are they on a rigid exercise regime or training for the annual walkathon?

3) Thinking back to eye contact, I don't make eye contact with people I pass by on the street because I feel they can cut me down to size and slander me with a single glance because I'm so vulnerable and timid. I also have this irrational fear that if I look at them they can read me. Eyes are the portal to the soul and I don't want my soul to be exposed. I realise this is most probably impossible considering that the majority of people are not psychically gifted.

4) Another flicker of my old pal Mr Disorientation. I amble forward, not really knowing my destination in town or why I was going wherever I was going. Sometimes I just lose my every bearing. Sometimes I am completely lost. Sometimes my Asperger's syndrome is a mystery to me. Sometimes I am a mystery to myself.

5) Yesterday being a total hate day, today not being so bad...although I am still being barged into by other students who think I'm nothing more than a weakling to be pushed around.

6) Hating shops such as Miss Selfridge, River Island and Topshop because of my colossal form.

7) Me being possibly the only person on the face of the earth to wear platformed shoes with a tracksuit.

8) Escaping into the nearby post office to avoid the mob of my ego-charged adversaries, then getting lumbered behind probably the slowest person in town. Why me? How come I always get trapped? Is it my Asperger's syndrome that's trapping me?

9) Area in which my locker is situated being constantly shrouded in darkness.

10) However not-so-terrible the day, I still dream of escape. Escape to where? Anywhere but here. Escape from my condition? Do I even want to escape from my condition?

11) The epidemic of mobile phones.

12) Pokèmon. They're everywhere I look! I'm having nightmares about the bloody things now!

13) Gorgeous boy who I seemed to be always encountering in the town library. (We've really got to stop meeting like this.)

14) Overhearing other people's conversations - how they come across as muddled.

Chapter 8
Friends

Haley

I am currently corresponding with another Asperger girl in Blackpool, Haley, who is morbidly depressed about her condition. She, like many other Asperger people, is very much misunderstood:

> *"No-one likes me, they all think I'm a psycho. I don't fit in anywhere, no matter where I go. I don't seem to be capable of making friends anymore either. I've never found anyone I can really relate to. I'm just this weird Generation X kid who sits around being petulant."*

In her letters, Haley constantly apologises for being a complete prat and for apparently annoying me. She says she is sorry for waffling on. Her deep-routed self-hatred is clear in every sentence she writes and she uses every opportunity to criticise herself:

> *"One of the main reasons I've taken so long responding is because once I realised you were a good person I found it frightening. I just have this idea that anyone I like hates me, or should hate me. I dunno, I'm just being stupid again I guess. Don't take any notice of me or encourage me, cos then I'll probably go away and stop annoying you."*

Like me, Haley has been moulded by her early experiences. She has been taught to feel worthless and pathetic and is unable to see how worthwhile a person she actually is. Due to the extent of her self-loathing, Haley is acutely paranoid and has also developed agoraphobia and claustrophobia which she is courageously battling against:

> *"This is so stupid: I've got both agoraphobia and claustrophobia! This summer, I stayed indoors for three weeks at one time because I got so scared of leaving my room. I was looking out the window seeing everything outside changing way too quickly and I just couldn't take it. I get the reverse at college. I think it's the desks. The first mock exam this year, I felt everyone was scrutinising me and when the teacher shut the door, I completely lost it and burst out the room within seconds."*

College is a nightmare for Haley, so she rarely turns up for all her lessons. She stresses how different she sees herself compared with the other students and how the selfish desire to be popular, which she despises, stili reigns supreme. Haley says she has been to four schools and has ruined her chances in them all and that college is the same:

"I know how you feel about the kids; they all seem to be scrambling for popularity with each other which just makes me feel like an outsider, so I then get more paranoid. I know it's a completely irrational paranoia, but I just seem to stand out from the other kids so much. Whenever I hear other kids having conversations, I get so pissed off. I want to kneecap them all, but it isn't worth it. I think they hate me enough already."

Haley's dislike for her peers doesn't, however, alter her perception of reality. She displays a very mature attitude about the way they treat her and reveals an astoundingly deep knowledge of human nature:

"I hate college but I don't worry about getting the piss ripped out of me or all the other kids hating me. You've got to expect them to join in with things like that - its only natural. When the 'in' crowd hate you, everyone else will, no matter what you do or don't do. People conform to the standards of the fashionable ones because they want to be popular. I think I deserve it anyway; if you were here you would see how I always act like a total prat. I've been a freak so long I really don't care what anyone says, because I'm used to it. Anyway, I just get so sick of all these narcissistic tossers, I actually want them to be abusive to me. At least then I know if they like me or not."

She shows her awareness again:

"I get really angry when people better off than me are upset, like they don't deserve to be. But I think humans have a way of making themselves unhappy anyway, so everyone gets upset sometimes. Most people are just insecure anyway. If everyone was secure in themselves there would be no point in Prozac."

Haley admits she does bizarre things - like shaking her head vigorously or stamping her feet - purely to attract attention, even though it's the wrong sort:

"The different reactions people give me are quite funny sometimes. I'm sitting in class and suddenly I start twitching my shoulders just to get

everyone to look at me. Sometimes I actually want them to think I'm a psycho for some dumb reason."

Despite having Asperger's Syndrome, Haley exhibits a very competent awareness of herself and others, and how she knows that her senses sometimes deceive her, when her paranoia is irrational, and how she has a tendency to over-dramatise:

"Do you ever feel like your problems are all just in your head? I know some of mine are, but that doesn't make them any less problematic."

Contrary to the common myth that Asperger people can't empathise, Haley appears to understand and relate to my problems perfectly. This could be because she is enduring them too, rather than just empathising. She is a very intelligent person and I believe that she can empathise because she tries to and because she wants to:

"You seem to feel quite guilty about things. Like you haven't earned the right to be upset or something? Correct me if I'm wrong, anyway, that's just my impression. Maybe I'm just thinking that because it's the way I feel. You think of Ethiopians eating leaves off trees and little kids in Sao Paolo getting shot in the head by cops then all your problems seem so trivial. But still, you can't dwell on conditions in the third world and things like that. I'm not saying we should all be self-pity-meisters, I just think you have the right to be upset and that shouldn't make you feel bad. There are always going to be people better or worse off than you for that matter. I'm sure you aren't a hypochondriac or digging for sympathy. I'm really sorry you feel that way. It's not really fair on someone like you I guess. The only good point could be one day you might get over it and then you'll have a better view of things. Sounds lame I know, but think of all the little perfect people who've never felt bad. They've never really experienced anything in the world either."

Haley presents a very cynical view of the world. However, given her situation, I believe she is entirely justified in feeling this way:

"Sometimes I think the whole world is completely fucked up. The worst part though, is that the only people who allow themselves to realise that are the ones who can't change anything. All the winners are happy, even if it's a corrupt system, it pays off for them, so no-one is complaining...bastards."

Haley admits to self-mutilation and self-inflicted sleep deprivation. Confused and emotionally unstable because no-one understands her, she resorts to torturing herself:

> "I just feel like I'm falling inside my own head. I'm not even myself. I just act like a complete zombie and I can rarely ever pull my real personality out of there. I want to go collapse somewhere, three hours sleep a night really isn't healthy. My eyes are both broken, they're into the bleeding stages now, since I hardly ever sleep. Talking of bleeding, I made a new painting with my blood today, which was about the only productive thing I did."

Suffering in silence?

Fortunately, not every case is as depressing as Haley's, but for the ones who are, life is not a life, it is an existence. It's a cold, unfriendly duration where no-one can understand you or make an effort to help you. So you stand alone, alienated from society and you suffer. Haley is just an example of how decent and reasonable Asperger people can be. There is nothing that warrants a nice person such as her to suffer like this. This is wrong. Neither Haley nor any other Asperger person deserves this treatment.

So how can you bring the Asperger person's peers to an understanding of this condition? And consequently, how can you get them to tolerate it and not to abuse the person who has it? The other crucial question to address here is: how can you raise an Asperger person's self-esteem, whether or not their condition is tolerated?

Any possible answers to these questions depend on several factors:
- Who is the 'you' in question?
- What is the age range and mentality of the peers in question?
- How much will your peers be willing to listen and learn?
- Is the Asperger person in question willing to be helped and to take advice?
- Will the Asperger person be willing to accept that he/she has problems?

Informing the peers

In my experience, trying to inform my peers of my condition has only reinforced my freak status. Very few people in my generation appear interested or concerned. Many of them accused me of lying to gain sympathy, and of gross exaggeration, but maybe this is just my misfortune? I always try to be accepting of advice and be aware that I have problems, but the majority of my peers prefer to remain ignorant of my condition.

I think that the motive behind their resistance to learn is that they want to see me as a freaky mainstreamer rather than a typical Asperger, because in that sense I am not allowed a syndrome to blame my freakiness on and am therefore just weird. I would assume the majority of my peers want to escape blame themselves - because more people will arise in defence of a registered disabled person (such as a Downs person, a blind person, a paraplegic person) than simply a freaky mainstreamer. They want to blame the person, not the syndrome.

A broad opinion of mine is that the majority of mainstreamers are compelled to conform to a particular set of standards, so it would seem obvious that anyone who didn't conform was maybe disobedient, stubborn or just plain abnormal, and somehow a lower rank of person with few rights and even fewer privileges. In general (although I cannot speak for every Asperger person) Asperger people don't conform, not because they want to defy convention, but because they don't realise or understand what convention is.

Why it is difficult for Asperger people to make and keep friends?

Many Asperger people are solitary types, either because they are content being this way or because they can't make or keep friends. I have never found it easy to make friends, which is why the friends I do have are so precious to me. In a strange sort of way, my Asperger's syndrome has been a useful selective tool. I might not be the most popular of people, but at least I know who really cares for me and who doesn't. Having taken an introspective view of myself, I am now able to see the cause behind me being socially inept, and if I was a mainstreamer I don't think I could tolerate the Asperger me. I'm not the most endearing person - not because I'm defensive and nasty, but because of my desperation for friendship. I try too hard to make friends, and mainstreamers recognise this and can detect my insecurity (and consequently my inferiority complex).

Generally, the mainstreamer's insecurity causes them to covert, which helps them where friendship is concerned. Asperger people, however, are exceptionally overt about their insecurity. It is written all over them, not just in their words, but in their actions, their expressions and the decisions they make. I don't really know how to explain this, but what I can say is that the insecurity barriers are evidently lower for an Asperger person when compared to a mainstreamer.

Insecurity is most noticeably displayed in the Asperger person's favourite topics of conversation - themselves and their interests/obsessions - whereas mainstreamers have a wider variety of conversational topics, so naturally, mainstreamers object to the limitations of Asperger conversation.

Also, the particular style in which Asperger people move - some very cautious and timid, others ranging from overly eager to forceful or aggressive - expresses their insecurity. So does that certain vulnerable look in their eyes (more obvious in some), and the way they might seem frightened, hesitant or hasty when making decisions. Their insecurity is found in those with a particularly stubborn nature, who always insist on having things their way - because (and I cannot emphasise this point enough) this is the only form of control and stability they can clutch at.

But mainstreamers, I believe (especially adolescents), crave security. My theory is that they associate themselves with secure people because it improves their confidence and disassociates themselves with insecure people because they dislike in them what they dislike in themselves. It is partly true that you reflect the company you keep, so hypothetically if your friends are self-assured and confident this will rebound onto you and, likewise, if they are insecure and lack that vital self-esteem. This is a major reason why it is difficult for me to make (and keep) friends - because often it is not what you look like, but how you behave that influences others opinions of you.

How to cope with losing friends

I reckon that almost everyone loses at least one friend during their lifetime - whether it's to death, irreconcilable differences, or purely loss of contact. I don't know if anyone else grieves over their lost friends like I have done. Initially, I suppose, they might be upset, but as time progresses and new friends emerge, the loss that was once felt will dissipate.

I, however, struggled to accept my losses. I never took the hint that people who were once my friends now disliked me because I didn't think there was anything to dislike about me in the first place. What is there to abhor in a person who does your homework for you, carries your bag to school, finishes the leftovers on your plate or donates their lunch money to you? How could anyone hate someone who would be their personal puppy dog?

The answer was staring me directly in the face. For a start, these so called friends were actually only opportunists using me for my devotion and services; so when I couldn't provide them with a new Barbie doll or a pretty gold locket they discarded me. For them I was a product to be used up and thrown away - worthless and ineffectual.

Secondly, real friends (rather than opportunists) don't want a doormat and I was the champion of doormat-ery. Rule No.1: don't be a doormat.

But whatever the reason, I refused to accept the impossibility of regaining my lost friends. I'd still phone them and when they would slam the phone down on me I'd just phone them right back (this procedure could happen up to 15 times with each ex-friend!). Being the naive, devastatingly insecure Asperger kid that I was, this all seemed perfectly natural to me. I'd use all my pocket money to buy my ex-friends lovely presents, hoping to win them back. Rule No.2: generous gestures won't work.

Ironically, my strategies for trying to retain friends were actually the reason I was losing them. What I really should have done was just get on with my life instead of pining over the past, and that's what I'd advise every other Asperger person who loses their friends to do. So Rule No.3: leave the past in the past, however much it might pain you.

Also, never neglect the fact that losing friends, however devastating it can be, is just another process of learning and growing up. You might not learn instantly, because everyone is different, but eventually you will, even if it's the 32nd friend you've lost. Rule No.4: accept it. Accept that friendship isn't seen through rose-tinted glasses, try not to repeat your mistakes (easy to say, not so easy to do - at first, that is), and constantly remind yourself how worthwhile you are and how much right you have to like yourself (also very difficult to do - I'm still trying, still slowly dragging myself up this steep hill, but I know that one day I'll reach the summit, in time).

Special friends for special people

Jodie has been my best friend for many years - my longest-known friend and one of the few genuine people I hold dear. We've known each other for ages and even though we went to different schools, out of school we were almost inseparable. We've always been close - Jodie was like all the friends I never had. We even call ourselves sisters. One of the first people Jodie confides in is me. That is why, when she first started out on her little clubbing adventures a few years back, I despised all the new friends she made with a vengeance. I was too scared of them to ever tell them this, though, although I told Jodie and my family. Back then, I didn't really understand about friendship because I was so socially ignorant. My parents called me overprotective, clingy, jealous, selfish, oppressive, stubborn, you name it - but with my limited knowledge (due to lack of experience) of friendship, I saw nothing wrong with my behaviour. I could easily admit to myself that this was the way I felt and that I wasn't in a hurry to change.

I didn't, however, behave like I was Jodie's mother by confining her to be in by such and such a time. In fact, I was exactly the opposite. I never objected to her going anywhere, as long as I knew she wouldn't get into any sort of trouble (although she's always been perfectly capable of handling precarious situations herself), yet I still felt protective towards her because of all that we've been through together - even though I knew I was about as much protection as tissue paper against a rainstorm.

Because her other friends and acquaintances confused my protective nature (they weren't exactly mistaken for doing so, when you think about it) with jealousy and stubbornness, they refused to associate with me. Whenever I saw them in town they would shun me, and Jodie was forced to divide her time between me and them. At least I never gave her an ultimatum. On the outside I can appreciate how Jodie's other friends felt - in their situation, faced with someone like me, I would have acted in the same way. But Jodie was my friend, and I just wanted her to remember that she was also one of the dauntingly few people I could ever trust and rely on. I had grown to be very emotionally insecure, and I needed some solidarity, just to keep me from taking that final step towards rigor mortis. That solidarity was Jodie. Despite going to separate schools we never lost our bond of friendship, and I would be damned if I lost her to a newer set of people. I can only praise her for tolerating me during those times, when I ruined so much of her fun by making her stay in with moody old me rather than go out and have fun with her confident bunch of fun-loving party animals.

As Jodie was like my other half, naturally, she was my opposite. She was the swan and I was the ugly duckling. She always tried to cheer me up and softened the blows of job rejections and cruel taunts. She tried to disguise my ugliness by putting it all down to low self-esteem, an immense persecution complex and even hallucinations when looking in the mirror, but I didn't see any point in metaphorically running away.

She would then say "Oh for God's sake! You can't be that bad!" And I would reply "Unfortunately I can, sorry. But who have I got to disappoint?" I would always argue with her about this, calling her a liar, I was so obstinate.

In contrast to my ugliness, Jodie was gorgeous. Blokes literally fell at her feet. She had so many boyfriends, I lost count. It was surprising she hadn't been spotted for a model agency yet. She could also blag her way into any job she wanted, and I mean any. She could apply herself to any situation and make good work of it, she could adapt to suit any requirements, an instant recipe for success. I was the opposite of all this.

The differences between us have often spurred rows. I used to say to myself "It's not every day you meet the embodiment of total female perfection, so why does Jodie choose to be my best friend? Why can't I have a pretty-but-fat friend instead?" Fortunately, I had learned that some thoughts were best kept to myself, so Jodie never heard me say this. And I'm glad she didn't. I always felt remorse after pondering over that question, hating myself for not appreciating her like I should.

Jodie has been my confidence and my motivation. Where I've been introvert, she's been extrovert. Where I've been quiet, she's been loud. Where I've been shy, she's been outgoing and gregarious. Where I've been self-conscious and paranoid, she's been confident and daring. She is like my other half, constituting the most vital part of my life and I don't know where I would be without her.

Finding acceptance

I'm known amongst my friends as Nita Nutcase. If you were to go out to a club or rave with me you'd see why. I'm a clubbing and raving fanatic (well, I would be if I had enough money to large it every weekend)! I've met many diverse people whilst out partying my lil' blue trainer socks off, the majority of which are perfectly amicable and hold no prejudices. That's how I've acquired most of my friends. Genuine friends who accept me as I am and actually like my strange way of thinking. To my friends I'm an eccentric and an individual, not a freak, nerd or weirdo. My friends are what real friends should be - caring, considerate, always willing to lend a hand whenever I'm in trouble. Words can't describe how much I appreciate and love them all and how grateful I am to them for rescuing me from a life of solitude.

It took me a while to find these friends though. Nothing is instant (apart from coffee). Those first few nights out on my own required bucketloads of courage and determination, as they would do for any loner who was new to the daunting world of clubbing. Even though the club I went to was situated in a relatively safe area, I didn't feel at all safe. Initially I felt paranoid and totally vulnerable, afraid to cast off my inhibitions and just have fun. I was terrified of being judged, having my every action under immense scrutiny by those around me. So I resigned myself to standing in the corner, looking my usual timid self. I was unhappy, lonely and afraid. I wanted to go home but knew I had to endure it up to 2 am. when my mum had agreed to pick me up.

Standing there alone, so conspicuous in my unflattering plus-sized tracksuit and grubby trainers, I was waiting on a miracle, praying on one. By some incredible twist of fate that miracle happened. It appeared in the form of Emma Offei ('Off-licence' to her friends). Like Jodie, Emma has always been a very gregarious and popular person, so why she chose to adopt me as her friend I really don't know. But hey, she adopted me right enough and I'm certainly not complaining!

Emma introduced me to her group of friends and from then on my social interaction broadened. Through Emma I met so many new and interesting people and gained enough confidence to finally start introducing myself, rather than having someone else do it for me. If it wasn't for Emma, I would never have met my wonderful ex-boyfriend Daley (who I still love to bits), or the crazy little pixie Anna (eats like a horse, body like a supermodel, grrr!), or the Sisters of Non-Sobriety Gemma and Becky - plus dozens of others.

Maybe I was just lucky...I can't be sure. What I do know, however, is that if a cowardly little nobody like me can strike gold once in a blue moon, other Asperger people can too - trust me. It's not easy, but it happened. There are many cruel people in this world but also many decent ones who are only too happy to befriend a loner. I'd just like to tell any Asperger readers that I was more timid than a lot of you, and I took that chance of going out. Everything carries a risk, particularly clubbing all on your lonesome, but in my case it was a risk worth taking.

Problems with friend's, friends and general social problems

A particular problem of mine is the issue of my friends. I'm stupefied by people who can just waltz into a new friend's party and come out with an address book's worth of new chums. My situation with Emma is exceptional - her friends welcomed me into their community - but with everyone else (Jodie, Kelly and various others who I've met along the way), it's identical; I just can't get along with their friends (or rather, only recently, they can't get along with me, seeing as I'm the one who's learnt to make all the effort?).

It's amazing how much variety there is in one circle of, say, four friends. The one who is my friend is broadminded and accepting, yet the other three are so dismissive of me. Maybe it's because they're unfamiliar with me - many people are cautious around newcomers and feel they need to secure their territory, as it were, and maybe they see me as posing a threat to their friendship with my friend? Perhaps it's due to my social skills which certainly leave a lot to be desired. (As mentioned before, I've learnt my conversational skills parrot-fashion and don't know much beyond the basic "Hi", "How are you?" , "So what's the story with you and Kelly?" , "What are your interests"? It's understandable that my limited conversation can deter people). Whatever the reason, my friend's, friends and I just clash. Here are a few diary extracts from previous years where I recall my thoughts and feelings about them:

March 2000

I can't figure Kelly's boyfriend John out at all. Sometimes he seems to like me, other times completely the opposite - you could almost say he was disdainful towards me. OK, so he wouldn't be without his reasons, but how do I know it's for those reasons he dislikes me? How come he won't just be honest and offer me some constructive criticism? If something about me annoys him, then he should tell me - at least I might be able to make amends then.

But no, he would rather just ignore and avoid me than voice his concerns - is that it? I don't know. I don't understand mainstreamers sometimes - I honestly feel like I'm from a different planet to them. I don't even know if he respects me. If he respected me he would be up-front and truthful with me. If I had to name one essential quality to my friends and family it would be giving honest advice where it's necessary. Be cruel to be kind - but only if you know it's in someone's best interests. I want John to advise me on how to amend this behavioural problem of mine, that's if it is me who has the problem. Maybe it's him? Perhaps he doesn't like me sitting here with him and Kelly like a goddamn gooseberry all the time, but that's my fault isn't it?

July 1998:

Went to a theme park with Amy and her friends from school. I thought Amy would be nice like she always is when it's just the two of us, but she was horrible. All she and her two friends did was insult me, never once trying to involve me in their conversation. They're such arrogant bitches to me! They treat me with no respect and make it perfectly clear I'm not wanted - as if I cramp their style and am unworthy of their elitist group's attention.

I have tried to relate to them but they just don't reciprocate. What did I do wrong? Is it that obvious just how abnormal I am? Or maybe I've misinterpreted the whole situation and meditated over hints which could have been purely accidental?
I don't know.

My lack of ability to comprehend people really frustrates me. I feel so stupidly lost. Do mainstreamers get this problem with their friend's, friends who they aren't really acquainted with, or is it specifically brain-impaired freaks like me?

I no longer speak to Amy any more. She chucked me out with the trash after that day, just cut me off without a word. I can guess why though - the 'in' crowd like Amy don't associate with the geeks like me, even if one of them might want to. From what I can gather, these people think and act as a collective and anyone who dares to disagree becomes an outcast. If you're not with them, you're against them.

I can't stress enough how much I hate conformity, snobbery and elitism. With hindsight I can see that I'm better off without Amy and her cronies, but sometimes I wonder if the story would be different had I been a mainstreamer who could adapt to the expectations of the group? But would I really want that? Would I truly be happy wearing a uniform all the time? Is that even what some friendships are all about, or have I misinterpreted it all? Would any psychoanalysts please raise their hand!

Less important because of my disability?

Since divulging my Asperger's syndrome I've really learnt who my friends are. When one of my (then) friends, Suzanne, found out, her opinion of me totally changed. She began to regard me like I was less of a person, less important, less trustworthy, less reliable, less real even; in that I mean she would ignore me half the time as if I just didn't exist. However, I had such low confidence then that I still grovelled at her feet, oblivious of the way she treated me. I knew that I had to keep friendship, and I would, no matter how humiliating it was...

Things got worse when she got together with Mark. Suzanne met her beau whilst out clubbing. The memory sticks so vividly in my mind, I can recall it like it was yesterday. Suzanne and I were eyeing up the talent on the dance floor whilst drinking Tia Maria and Cola at the bar. Mark had sauntered over to Suzanne and had pinched her bum from behind, making her swirl round in surprise. I was instantly jealous - that sort of thing would never happen to me.

They had hit it off instantly and I was discarded like a broken camera, which was exactly what I felt like. I was a memory of good times for Suzanne, but now she had the opportunity to have even better times by purchasing a super-advanced photo-system with easy-to-load film and all-that-digital-stuff. In short, I was a rhinestone and Mark was a sapphire. He was a mainstreamer and I had Asperger's syndrome, but that didn't mean I had no feelings. Asperger people feel too, some of us more so than mainstreamers. We just feel differently, somehow. I can't really explain it.

They had wandered off together that night, leaving me running around like a dumbfounded headless chicken, scouring every inch of the overcrowded club for them and bawling my eyes out. After thoroughly humiliating myself, I left. Fortunately, Suzanne's house was only a mile away from town. I ran all the way back to Suzanne's house and hammered on the door, drenched with rain and seething. The lights were on and when I pressed my ear to the door I could hear noises, but no-one answered. I knocked again, but still no reply. They were in there right enough, but they just didn't want me around. I had started bawling again, crouching down to open the letter box and screaming through it like an infant, until they finally let me in. Suzanne had rushed to the door with nothing else on but Marks' coat, angrily ordering me up into her bedroom. She told me to stay there until she said otherwise.

I was such a shy, timid thing that I wouldn't dare argue with her, so I trudged straight upstairs and into Suzanne s room, remembering not to sit on the bed - "I'll strangle you if you sit on my bed!" she had yelled after me. So, whilst I sat on the blue carpeted floor, still sobbing, I was once again visited by the Brain Invaders (aka the B.I. - wayward thoughts and self-deprecation). The B.I. said it would have been all right if Suzanne and Mark had called the club to tell me they wanted their privacy, so I could have got a bus back home. But no, they were too engrossed in each other to even think of that.

After a mammoth two hours my bladder was bursting, but I was too terrified Suzanne would hear me plodding along the hallway to do anything about it. So I just sat there, praying I wouldn't wet my knickers (for a long, long time now, I've had an incontinence problem). I was finally given the go-ahead when Suzanne and Mark appeared at the door and ordered me out. They emerged an hour or so later and saw me slouched on the settee, watching telly like a pathetic loner on a night when I should have been out having a good time. They had such massive grins on their faces that I felt even more embarrassed than I had done when I got in. I had never felt so low. They knew I was a muppet, I knew I was a muppet, the entire town knew I was a muppet. I summoned up all my courage and, in a trembling voice, asked Suzanne if she thought my condition affected my emotions at all. She had replied "well it has to, or else you wouldn't have it." Then I asked her if she thought she could abuse my friendship like that. She said "Oh come on, you're retarded! You know f*** all about friendship!" And there it was. Suzanne had affirmed that now I had a label on me, I had been demoted to second-class citizenship. I had burst out crying and Suzanne and Mark had gone out again, leaving me alone in the house. Suzanne's mum had returned home at 11pm and found me huddled in a corner, rocking. I know now that Suzanne was never a genuine friend anyway, so I'm better off without her. But that memory still hurts and despite that experience, I let similar things happen to me time and time again - because I had believed Suzanne. I had believed I really was a second-class citizen.

My problem was that I was very gullible, but fortunately, this is different now. I've still got my gullible tendencies but a lot less than I used to. I think it was basically a learning process. However, because of my condition, it just took longer than usual. Now I'm aware that I've got just the same rights as everyone else, and that I don't have to stand for that sort of treatment.

Having Asperger's syndrome does not make me less human, less emotional, but simply more vulnerable. So I conclude that other Asperger teenagers like myself should always be forewarned of the problems they can and will encounter with mainstreamers. Parents - talk to your kids; and kids - listen to your parents! I didn't...and see what happened to me.

Chapter 9
My All-Inclusive Asperger Package

Problems with understanding language

Are there any definite answers to the mysteries that are innuendoes, hints and inferrals? Language is this immensely complex matter to me, like an ever-evolving maze which I am caught in and cannot escape from. It frightens me that I don't understand it. I think sometimes language can be too diverse for me to grasp properly. Whether this is due to my condition actually preventing me from doing so or not I can't be sure, but I know I've got this sort of mental block when it comes to analysing the way mainstreamers use words. It's not because I'm incompetent though.

Due to my limited comprehension of language, I frequently feel alienated and trapped. In a society where so many others can easily prosper, I am perpetually struggling, although I realise that not everyone prospers, even if they may appear as if they do. I also know I'm not entirely alone in my predicament, even though sometimes I feel like I am. There's a glimmer of hope somewhere and I won't rest until I find it. I'll read more literature about my condition, I'll do some more soul searching, I'll talk to the specialists, I'll have any tests (brain scan? Aura analysis? Tarot cards? Crystal ball?) - but eventually I'll make it through.

Colour coding

Ever since I was a child I've been obsessed with organisation and structure. One of the ways I expressed this was through colour coding. However, this was more so before than now. My obsession with colours began at a very early age, resulting from a dislike of the carpet, which was a vast, multicoloured and multi-patterned expanse of bristle-fibre. Being able to concentrate on only one colour at a time, I was completely phased by the carpet and I remember feeling nauseated when looking at it from the stairs, seeing all those colours and patterns swimming in front of me.

Because of that carpet, I always associated multi-colour with confusion and dizziness. I even opted out of the school visit to see *Joseph and the Amazing Technicolour Dreamcoat!* That was why I became a Mrs Mono-Colour Extrordinaire. And believe me, I really went to town on that one! I would wear only one colour and carry accessories in only that colour. I'd even paint my shoes that colour, because my mother couldn't afford to buy a pair of shoes for every colour of the rainbow and all their various shades. Plus, everything had to be specific.

If I wore a light blue sweater, then I couldn't wear dark blue trousers or royal blue shoes - every item would have to be light blue. At the time, I couldn't understand why so many people laughed at me on non-uniform days at school and pointed at me in town. It seems funny now, when I look back, though - I mean, you hardly see a kid throwing a tantrum because their t-shirt is a fraction of a shade different from their jumper do you? But I was like that. You could almost have called me multi-colour phobic. I also used to stick coloured labels on things. There was a yellow sticker on my underwear drawer, a red one on my pyjama drawer and a blue one on my sock drawer. My dolls were housed in pink boxes, my school books in green ones. The clothes in my wardrobe were organised into colour coded sections, likewise with my shoes. However, if you think about it, colour coding is a very practical device. It's like a filing cabinet, but instead of placing things under A-Z, they are under colours. So no-one can say I was totally without reason.

Nowadays, however, I only colour code my work, because otherwise the separate topics within each subject would get mixed up. The change didn't suddenly spring upon me, it was more of a natural progression. Over the years I just slipped out of this obsession and grew to ignore the carpet - although when I get my own place the carpet definitely won't be multicoloured!

Another common myth - honesty

It has been said that Asperger people (most commonly youngsters) are brutally honest and that they don't know how to lie. However, from my personal angle, I don't entirely agree with this opinion. For a start, it's a broad generalisation and, by principle, I'm always very sceptical towards these things - kind of a contradiction in terms seeing as I use them myself and there is no viable excuse to get me out of this one, other than the feeble "I don't like them but I use them only when there is no alternative", but again, for the billionth time, I digress...

The honesty part is true to an extent, but is it directly linked with, or determined by, the inability to deceive? Not in my case (I can only speak from personal opinion here). Until I had left primary school, I was hopeless at keeping secrets and would blurt out my honest feelings to my immediate family. I once said "You're horrible!" to a group of peers at school then they beat me up for it, so after that I was too afraid to speak my feelings to them. If my mother wore a perfume I didn't like, I wouldn't hesitate to let her know! When she had her hair permed I told her to march right back to the hairdressers and get it reversed, because I thought it made her look like a poodle and that everyone would be shouting "Fifi La Pew!" at her in the street (Fifi La Pew was actually a cartoon skunk, by the way, but in my opinion the name just had poodle written all over it!). So yes, in all fairness, I was ruthlessly honest. However, this wasn't to say I couldn't lie. Fair enough, I was a hopeless liar too, but at least I knew how. On the other hand, I can't deny that I saw the BBC2 programme *The Science of Lying* and watched psychological experiments with Autistic (not Asperger) children which added weight to the incapability of lying theory.

A professor (the name escapes me) conducted the Little Red Riding Hood and the Wolf experiment, where Little Red Riding Hood was being chased by Mr Wolf and hid in a cave near her Grandma s house. Naturally, Mr Wolf should assume Lil Red would be in the house, but he decides to ask the children that were participating.

The mainstream children saw that Lil Red's life depended on them, so they lied, saying that she was in the house. The Autistic children, however, really couldn't get their head round lying, even though it was clear that Lil Red would end up dead if they didn't.

Was this because they couldn't understand the severity of the situation? That maybe, because it wasn't a real incident they didn't really have to save Lil Red's life, so lying was not necessary? In my opinion, no. I've always been under the impression that many Autistic (rather than Asperger) children couldn't distinguish between fantasy and reality and that they would do the same in a real situation as they would in a fantasy one. I think that most Autistic children just don't have the capacity to lie. If the children had Asperger's syndrome, maybe the results would have been different. I know that an Asperger characteristic is irrespective honesty and that a predominantly Autistic one is the inability to lie, which certainly connects the two. I can understand how some people might think an Autistic idiosyncrasy is applicable to everyone under the Autistic spectrum, so consequently it would make sense that if Autistic children can't lie, then Asperger children cannot either. And yes, maybe this is true for some Asperger youngsters. I have no evidence to the contrary.

I have therefore concluded that there is a difference between the ability to lie and the ability to deceive, and that this is what separates Autistic from Asperger. By definition, Autistic children can't lie, whereas Asperger children can, but they cannot deceive.

Motor clumsiness

These form an integral part of my life, affecting me in so many ways. I cannot thoroughly express all of them. Also known as an absence of co-ordination, motor clumsiness is associated with a range of development disorders, and is particularly synonymous with Asperger's syndrome. I am a prime example of this. Despite being a very early developer puberty-wise - seven years old - I was certainly at a concerning age before I could walk, talk or write at all. I was a late walker, still crawling at two years old. Balancing was a huge problem - my bike had stabilisers until I was 11. But learning to walk was the worst. Never thinking of using my arms to help me, my upper body always remained stiff, as if my arms were sewn to my sides. I found tandem walking (placing one foot in front of the other as though I were treading a tightrope) impossible, so I developed this odd gait - waddling like a duck or a human with severe bladder problems. This was only one of the many reasons my peers found for bullying me.

One of Clare Sainsburys' interviewees, Karen, offered a paragon description of PE, calling it the 'nemesis' of her life and the 'ultimate in social embarrassment'. Like most Asperger individuals, sports and co-ordination were immensely challenging for me, and still are. Ball games were a big no no, not just because my hand-eye co-ordination was terrible, but also because I had a genuine phobia of anything that didn't have wings and flew, due to me being smacked in the face at full force with a football on my first day at primary school. Whenever the object flew towards me I would duck or dodge out the way, often tripping over my feet and landing in a tangled heap on the ground and providing my peers with an easy source of amusement. Even when, at about age eight, I overcame my phobia, I still couldn't ever catch, throw, hit or kick a ball. At my school, the sports activities were always integrated, meaning that the girls were allowed to play football, baseball, basketball, rugby and cricket, and the boys netball and hockey. Needless to say, I was invariably the last one picked for any team sport. In fact, I had to sit on the sub's bench most of the time because the kids would complain so much when the teacher assigned me to their team. I was certainly banned from playing table tennis because, with a maximum of four players, you've got a much higher chance of losing than with football or hockey. The teams were honestly better off without me, because of another reason. I was oblivious to any sort of rules, whether written, spoken, or unspoken. It wasn't so much a failure to understand at all, but a general misunderstanding. I understood each rule separately, but en-mass they just brought confusion, and I would get one rule muddled up with another. For example, in netball the rules of who was where and who threw to whom baffled me, and I would end up thinking I could simply throw the ball in any direction and just hope it would gravitate towards anyone else in my team (I never succeeded in catching the ball, so I was unable to put this theory into practice).

Swimming troubled me, too. I hated the feel of water in my face and surrounding my flabby body and not being able to touch the floor or sides. I cried to my mother that every swimming pool should have an arm rail for people to hold on to. I would certainly have felt more encouraged to get in the pool then. Where there was only water. I could find no tangible structure to cling to, implying a loss of control. I was literally out of my depth. I'm fine with swimming now though, in fact, I really enjoy it. I can't remember exactly when the change came because it was a very gradual thing.

I had a speech impediment up until about age six and I couldn't form sentences until about age four. I would also sometimes speak and write backwards, as if it was totally natural, for example: kuy lems elttob klim (milk bottle smell yuck) was one of my favourites, which was indicative of my dyslexia. Quite a few people thought I was actually speaking in a foreign language. Unfortunately I lost that talent in my first year of primary school, but I'll never forget it. In relation to this I also developed several involuntary muscle spasms and facial tics, which I was perfectly aware of and taught myself how to prolong them and do them backwards. My handwriting posed a significant cause for concern. Up until about age 10, it was thoroughly incomprehensible. It was perfectly legible to me, but to everyone else it was simply a mess of scribbles. I held my pencil in a fist for a considerably long time, which was a large part of the problem.

Due to me having no registered physical handicap (I was always defined as simply a late starter), everyone else interpreted it as messiness or stupidity. Dictation terrified me, because I was not only a messy writer, but also a very slow one. I would be only half-way through a sentence when the teacher would bellow out the next one. The classroom became my home at break and lunch times, when I was made to stay in and finish all my uncompleted work. In her book 'Martian in the Playground' Clare Sainsbury states that even as an adult, she still can't do joined up handwriting and that by trying to she ended up printing the letters very close together. The same applies to me. I've finally conceded that I can't join my letters so, like Clare, I simply print them very close together instead.

Problems with manual dexterity accompanied this. I just couldn't grasp the ability to use both hands simultaneously. Knives and forks were a nightmare, dressing myself was a whole assault course in itself, and anything involving the act of tying or weaving was impossible. My mother had to make me special clip-on ties for school, because I could never tie them myself, and when my shoelaces were undone they stayed undone until someone else corrected them! I mostly always had a packed lunch because I could eat that with my fingers (I had to drink yoghurts through a straw, because holding a yoghurt pot with one hand and a spoon with the other was very confusing), but it wasn't a pretty sight. I got picked on countless times because I ate like a baby, stuffing food into my mouth and wiping the excess on my bulging cheeks. In every situation, whether it involved utensils or fingers, my table manners were atrocious. Fortunately, that has been rectified now, so feel free to invite me round to tea anytime!

Accents and sub-personalities

On the phone to my friends, I am usually just Nita the Glasdonian (hybrid Dundonian/ Glaswegian), but when I go out anywhere (day or night) I can be anyone from Nita the Essex bird to Nita the scouser, Nita the shaftie (someone from Belfast), Nita the sack of tomatoes (Sacramento) Californian or even Nita the nonspecific ozzie. When asked "why do you speak in so many different accents when you go out?" I replied "because I get bored easily and I don't feel comfortable in any one accent for long." The reason behind this is that I don't know who I really am, where I'm from, or what I believe in. Every accent feels real and false at the same time. I am never entirely happy in any accent, even if it's my real one (which is an amalgamation of several accents in itself, due to my easily-influenced personality). A lot of people say I take on different personalities when I change my accents, that I am more confident when I'm a scouser; genial when I'm a Californian; more laid-back when I'm an ozzie; more apprehensive and vulnerable when I'm just me, but I've never really noticed this. I certainly don't think I suffer from split personality syndrome, but other people have commented on a few differences in my demeanour that I cannot see. I feel like the same me in one accent as I do in another. The same way I feel the same me in baggy sports gear as I do in formal wear or club wear. I may be happier physically and emotionally wearing trainers than platformed heels, but my mindset is no different. I cannot really explain further than that. If I myself felt that putting on a different accent would make a positive difference, then I could elaborate, but that's not the case.

Influence and influenced

In my opinion there are two types of Asperger people: those who influence others and those who are influenced by others. I don't necessarily think being an influence on others is better than being influenced, it all depends on your circumstances really. Aspergers such as Einstein have had a positive influence on our way of thinking and, although he is not to everyone's liking, Bill Gates is undeniably instrumental in the world of computer technology. In her autobiography 'Pretending to be Normal' Liane Holliday-Willey explains how, at school, her differences enabled her to be a leader rather than a follower. Most Asperger people I have encountered, however, have been of the latter kind, of which I am one. If the influence is positive then this is no problem but, unfortunately, I have yet to encounter one Asperger person who has not been negatively influenced. Maybe because most Asperger people (especially youngsters and teenagers) are highly impressionable, they are unable to see the difference between right and wrong. This was certainly the case for me. I would never have done anything with malicious intent, but because I didn't have the slightest notion that what I was doing was wrong, because I couldn't see where my actions were leading or the consequences they would have, too many bad things have happened to me and those around me.

Personally, I would prefer to be influential rather than influenced any day. Despite what I just said about influence being equally as positive as it can be negative, I continuously feel like such a sheep - so dependent. I have this theory that there is a real me in my brain somewhere, locked up inside some hidden section, just waiting to be set free. The real me is the person I aspire to be, the one who sets the trend instead of following it, the renegade who can stand alone and not feel scared, who can hold her own and be strong in times of adversity. I know it is possible to find her and to exert a positive influence on others, but I don't know where to start looking.

Arguments and blame

My relationships with people have always been volatile, especially ones with family members. I can appreciate how tough it is for them having to deal with me and I respect them for their persistence, but half the time it seems like they're trying to put me on a guilt trip and that I should be apologising for having this condition (I don't know if this is actually true, but it's just the impression I get). That angers me, because sometimes I feel like I'm being unfairly punished, serving a sentence for a crime I didn't commit. Also, because I'm the abnormal one in the family, I'm always made to feel I'm the one to blame for everything that goes wrong. My condition makes me a target for blame (and sometimes ridicule, when my parents are particularly angry), because it's much easier to rebuke the person with obscure traits, few manners and little social understanding, than it is the socially-apt mainstreamer. I'm far from perfect, but I can't be wrong all the time. My mother is a very proud woman who believes she is incapable of doing wrong. I would even call her self-righteous, and when her saintliness or moral fibre is questioned she launches into Operation Livid Defence and refuses to back down until she gets a proper apology. As for my father, well, he's just a sheep in these incidents. Anyway, my parents aren't the most tolerant of people, so it's very easy to provoke them. I don't do this intentionally, but they accuse me of it and that's when I snap back. I like to think my fuse is slightly longer than my parents but, admittedly, when I'm in the wrong mood I can be just as easily provoked and I'll flip. When I'm extremely angry I degenerate into a crockery throwing, foul-mouthed and even more foul-tempered psycho, but fortunately this doesn't happen as much as it used to. My parents always want to win arguments so if I scream at them they scream back even louder. They say they're copying my example, to show me how ridiculous I am, but in my opinion they're just lowering themselves to my level. Maybe if they used the calm approach they would get through to me. I've advised them about this countless times, but being the dogmatic creatures that they are, my advice falls on deaf ears. They're basically very childish, insecure people at heart, which is their reason for adopting this high-and-mighty stance. Like many mainstreamers, pretence is their stability.

Is it only Autistic people who reject this facade, opting for honesty and bearing their true character instead? Is it our honesty that makes us a target for abuse? In my honest opinion, I'd have to say yes. When my parents and I argue, our arguments could top the Richter scale! They accuse me of having a temper control problem, yet they're too negligent of their own temper control. I love my parents, but I hate their hypocrisy. They have got as much of a temper problem as me, but until they accept it, I don't think the arguments will stop.

Controlling my temper

I had no fuse at all when I was a child, you could wind me up like a clockwork toy and I'd go completely ballistic, but nowadays I'm different (most of the time). If things anger me now I don't charge around the room fuming, red in the face, with steam shooting out of my ears and nostrils. Instead, I apply the tactics my best friend and mentor Jodie taught me - to distract my anger by concentrating on something else for a minute, for example my studies, my music or my novels, and then returning to the problem and trying to solve it. It's honestly true that after this, the problem doesn't seem half as bad as it did before because I can put it in perspective. You've probably heard about this tactic many times before, but maybe you dismissed it and wrote it off because it sounded ridiculous. I thought it was stupid to begin with. I can only say try it out, because it works for me, and I'm not the easiest of people to please! I find it simple yet very effective. Remember that it did not come naturally to me, and it's highly unlikely that it will for other Asperger people. Jodie devoted a considerable amount of time training me how to apply it because, in my honest opinion, any new concept is quite difficult for an Asperger person to grasp. However, if after applying the tactics, the problem hasn't already lessened, or if it can't be solved, then admittedly sometimes I get mad and break stuff, but this is comparatively rare to how I used to be. Plus, everyone loses their calm occasionally - It's human nature.

Naivety

It's not uncommon for Asperger youngsters to develop, psychologically, much later than mainstreamers. Many are naive and have no understanding of the bad things in this world. I know two Asperger teenage girls who have been raped and many Asperger youths who receive the blame for their companions' wrong doings. One girl had to take the rap for stealing a few CDs, even though it was her so-called friends who were to blame. I have met many others who have been victims of unprovoked attacks, both verbal and physical. All of them were in their mid to late teens and none of them understood why they had been taken advantage of and started on.

Here is one incident from my 1998 diary (note this was before Amy shunned me), detailing my thoughts and, most importantly, my naivety:

> Amy bought a jesters hat at the school fair and told me to wear it. She was doing me a favour by letting me stay round her house till 8pm so it was only fair I should do something for her in return. So I wore it, thinking what harm can it do...
>
> Amy and her 19-year-old brother Wayne drove to a hardware store to buy two funnels and a metre of plastic tubing to make beer bongs out of. I've never received so many weird stares in my life, but they weren't amused stares, they were 'you're a freak so get the hell outa town' stares. I heard them sniggering behind my back all the time and couldn't figure out why. I walked past a man with a chin piercing, briefly glancing at him.
>
> "Got a f***ing problem?!" he spat at me.
>
> Well excuse me! That's the second time I've almost been started on today you know. I don't give a monkey who insults me, because everyone insults me, but the eagerness of so many people to start a fight certainly strikes a chord of anxiety.

With hindsight, I realise why this happened. It doesn't take a devious James Bond villain to know that wearing a bright orange jesters hat attracts attention, usually the wrong sort. I was only being ridiculed because of the hat. It would have been the same for any stranger with a bizarre accessory, but I couldn't see that. Amy had set me up, plain and simple, and I honestly couldn't see it, I was that naive. And why? For a start, even after enduring years of bullying, I still held the belief that the sinners would reform. I believed that Amy, who had once bullied me mercilessly, had reformed, for the simple fact that now she was associating with me on a regular basis. I had some crazy misconception that this constituted a friend. Secondly, I thought there was one rule for everyone. That if the 'in' crowd could wear furry coats and day-glow clothing, then I could wear a luminous orange hat with bells dangling from it. The in crowd could step as far out of line as they wanted, but the freaks couldn't deviate from it even one inch without being derided. I wouldn't have been bothered if the hat was solely responsible for the taunts, but it wasn't the hat they were mocking, it was me and neither hell nor high water could rouse me to smell the coffee.

With regards to my miscomprehension of 'the eagerness of so many people to start a fight', I now realise that my naivety again prevented me from seeing the bad in people. I was anxious because I didn't understand how nasty people could be, and this coming from a person who had been the butt of classroom jokes and victim of playground torments. How could I have been so blind? To any parents of Asperger children, I'd instruct you to be cruel to be kind. If possible, have regular discussions with your child about the cruel side of their peers, make them aware that society is as much a nasty place as it a nice one. There will always be kids who, if given the opportunity, will abuse them and walk all over them, because a naive kid is a vulnerable kid.

I'm not entirely blaming my parents, but they didn't ever tell me about the wicked ways of the children's world. Maybe they thought this was in my best interests, that by keeping me innocent they were protecting me? Maybe they thought the awful truth would contaminate my impressionable young mind? I don't know, I've never asked them. What with my Autistic behaviour, bullying would have most probably been an issue anyway, but if I'd had due warning then maybe things might have been different? If I'd been prepared...But enough of the what if's. If Hitler had won the war, we would all be speaking German. If Nostradamus had been right, you wouldn't be reading this book by now.

A lot of Asperger youngsters have an exceptionally innocent and naive outlook on the world. It's difficult for them to understand the emotional complexity of dislike and hate, so why people argue, bully, jeer, taunt, fight, maim and kill is beyond their comprehension. This was certainly true for me. Up until I started secondary school I thought the grass was greener everywhere else in the world and that I had just been placed in an unfortunate situation which God, or my own alien race, would rescue me from. I disregarded the news and the headlines so, when aged 12, making a conscious effort to sit through 30 minutes of news bulletins, I saw brutality, war and murder, I was mortified. That part of my mentality acts as a sort of conscience for me. Nowadays I am accepting of the way the world is. It still troubles me a little bit but, nonetheless, I've learned how to take reality.

Naivety and innocence aren't flaws, just misconfigurations in the Asperger's brain. Asperger people don't choose to view the world through rose-tinted glasses, it's just an inherent trait a lot of them share. The majority of them don't know any different, having been absorbed in their own perfect fantasy world, so when their fictional time-bomb explodes and they hear the shrill ring of their factual wake-up call, it's like being plunged into the fiery chaos of hell. This is why, if my fantasy world hadn't dissipated by now, that part of my brain would revile against clubland animosity. The concepts of rivalry and bravado would also be tough to tackle, as would the concept of solidarity by brute force, because I wouldn't have been able to delve into the psychological realms of insecurity.

It is insecurity that compels people to form allegiances, to boast and argue and pick fights, and it is the driving force behind the music wars. Many people think that insecurity can be vanquished by being part of a group and by having a sense of belonging, conforming to a particular set of standards, but it cannot. Conformity is also a concept which evaded my brain as a youngster, which is the reason why I do not confine myself to a specific core music.

But there is one last thing - the most vital component of all that is commonly lacking from the Asperger's brain. In order to understand why clubland disputes break out, you must first understand that partner insecurity goes hand in hand with a lack of respect. At the end of the day, carefree clubbing comes down to the fundamental morals of respect. The majority of people respect others in clubs, on the streets and in society in general, so it doesn't matter what music you like as long as you have this respect. A lack of it damages a happy atmosphere. I'm just thankful that I came to my senses before I started clubbing!

My needs and wants

Nita's Hierarchy of Needs:

- I want to be confident within myself - to be sure I could hold my own in an argument, even if I don't win
- When I lose I want to be a gracious loser
- I want to rid myself of this pessimistic approach I have to life, because it's only going to hinder me. As well as having Asperger's syndrome, I also suffer from bipolar disorder (see Chapter 12) which plays a massive part in dictating my emotions
- I want to maintain friendships
- I want to be able to like myself - Asperger's syndrome, underactive thyroid, bipolar disorder and all
- I want to be confident and positive about my life
- I want to get a good job and be able to live independently, without having to worry about finances
- I want to muster the power to accept myself and all my faults
- I need to be understood and I need to understand others
- I need to be tolerated and I need to be able to tolerate others who are similarly annoying
- I need to know if I should blame myself for everything that's bad in my life
- I need, not want, reassurance that I'm liked because I'm very insecure.

Self Amendment

No, it's not that easy to expel
The pain inside,
Despite all my protective walls
There are some things
I can't hide.
There's a distant morning -
A purity that's free,
But confined
Within this prison
It's something I can't see.
My mind's a raging torrent,
There's fire within my eyes,
I'm battling
With myself again,
I have to realise.
Confused and tormented
By the demons in my head,
Telling me I'm always wrong,
And there's another
Path to tread.

So I write a letter of apology and address it to myself, it reads:

I know
It's not that easy to expel
The pain inside,
But I don't need these
Protective walls
Because I admit,
I cannot hide.
There's a distant morning -
A purity that's free,
Mine
When I break these chains
Mine
When I can see.
I'm sorry
That I've hurt you,

There's fire within your eyes,
Forgive me for my trespasses
For now I realise.
Confused no longer
By the demons in my head,
I know now
Where I went wrong,
And can find the right
Path to tread.

A Public Apology

Forgive me if:
I'm too ready to please,
I act the fool,
I'm down on my knees -
Praying aloud to God above
That you would show me
Some sort of love.

Forgive me if:
I stand out from the crowd,
I look conspicuous,
I shout too loud,
I'm slow on the uptake,
I'm callous or rude,
I interrupt, intervene or intrude.

Forgive me if:
I laugh when I should cry,
I'm too curious and always asking why,
I'm too enthusiastic, eager as a child,
I'm weird, abnormal, insane or wild.

And if you can't,
Then, in the immortal words of Eric Cartman:
"Screw you guys,
I'm going hoooooome!"

Chapter 10
Social Activities

The Social Skills Pilot Group

During the last two weeks of November and the first two of December 2000, I attended a social skills group set up by Essex Social Services. It was a twice weekly schedule, consisting of four teachers and seven other Asperger pupils. I don't know whether the teachers were specially selected for this scheme or were involved voluntarily, but each of them proved very successful in relating to the Asperger group. They were friendly, open-minded and inquisitive, always encouraging the group to talk and express themselves. They had also devised a clever strategy for keeping the hyperactive ones among us under control. One of them took the manic kid out the room and talked calmly to him/her until the hyperactivity had subsided, then returned to the room again. They never said a harsh word to us, or raised their voices, or reprimanded us. If we didn't want to join in then they didn't force us to and they set the work at a very gradual pace so that no-one felt pressured. Needless to say all the work was completed!

Teachers and pupils

I love meeting fellow Asperger youths and never cease to be amazed at how individual each one is. Sometimes it's easy to forget individuality when you're studying a certain group of people and it's understandable to assume that those who share certain characteristics can differ so vastly personality-wise.

I met one 13-year-old boy, Dylan, who had an exceptional talent for character art, yet was too shy to even utter his name. When we (the group) were introducing ourselves, Dylan pulled his hat over his eyes and hugged his knees, shivering. He refused to move from his chair until leaving time, shaking his head whenever anyone spoke to him. Looking after Dylan required utmost patience - the teachers did a fantastic job. From observing the many diverse characters of the group, I can truly comprehend how monumental a task looking after Asperger youngsters is. There was the silent, shy but obstinate Dylan; two highly excitable boys, Gary (14) and Mikey (11), who would run riot if given the chance; me, who could talk till the cows came home; Bill (16) who was twitching and muttering to himself constantly; Crispin (18), who was reluctant to participate; Kathy (17), also with Tourette's Syndrome and an occasional tendency to do things on impulse (such as getting a drink, standing up or hurrying off); and finally Sara (16) who was overcome with nerves. All very amicable people right enough, but challenging to get through to half the time - especially me when I'm in Full Rant Ahead mode!

Of course, these teachers were a lot more tolerant than most of the teachers the group had encountered at school, which is why I feel the scheme was so successful. They gave everyone a chance, never discriminating against the more challenging pupils. Nothing seemed to phase them (or if it did, then they disguised it well). They worked with us rather than burdening work on us. They spoke with us rather than to us.

The syllabus

Each session the group worked through different subjects. The first session consisted of everyone introducing themselves then being organised into two groups of six, where we wrote down and annotated a few important points about ourselves, such as:

- Who we were
- Where we stayed/lived
- Who the important people in our lives were
- What others have described us as
- What our interests were
- What our dreams were
- Who decided things in our lives
- What we would like help with.

I found it all really interesting, not to mention helpful, when we brainstormed all our ideas and compiled lists, because it added so much more clarity to everyone's character. Everyone was encouraged to contribute and to speak their feelings, we were made able to see each other as individuals, rather than Asperger case studies.

There were certain common interests amongst the group. We all had hobbies, all loved both *Austin Powers* films, and were all avid watchers of *Father Ted* and *South Park*. Some of us were collectors - I collected key-rings, Mikey collected wrestling paraphernalia, Bill collected mobile phone covers (an astounding 88 in total) and Crispin collected stamps and sugar packets. Strangely enough, I collected a grand total of 144 salt packets from around the globe when I was nine and numerous ketchup and barbecue sauce sachets. I also used to collect plastic knives and forks.

The 'What we would like help with' was especially useful. It not only reinforced the problems characteristic of the condition which we all shared, e.g. making and keeping friends, improving our confidence, defending ourselves, making the distinction between jokes and insults, but also provided a comprehensive insight into the varying needs of Asperger people. Some wanted practical help, such as how to construct a website and how to build a robot; others craved emotional advice, such as how to relate to our families and how to stop hating ourselves.

Friendships

We brainstormed what we thought friendships meant. The teachers helped us come to the conclusion that friendship was a two-way process of giving and receiving and of mutual respect and trust. It didn't necessarily mean shared interests or agreeing with everything they said, but an overall respect for their opinions. Most of my previous friendships had been all about me giving and my so-called friends taking advantage of my naivety. With a lot of other Asperger people, however, it's all about taking and giving nothing back in return. This is not because Asperger people are selfish, it's because they simply don't understand the ingredients that make a friendship.

The key skills required in a friendship are listening, turn-taking and making sure you know what was said. It's very easy to misinterpret what people say, so it's important to go over things in your head or ask your friend outright if you have any doubts. This may sound stupid but, trust me, it's prevented countless arguments in my case. If your friends don't agree with this method and call you stupid, then to be honest they weren't real friends in the first place - that's what it all boils down to. Here are the group's suggestions about how to tackle this:

1) Ask them to repeat themselves
2) Could you explain that in a different way?
3) Am I right in thinking that you mean this?
4) Ask them to tell you more about it
5) Slooooooow doooowwwwn! (only if you're good friends with them!)
6) Adopting an inquisitive expression, in case you're stuck for words
7) Hmm, that's an interesting concept...
8) Question them in more detail
9) Go about it the humorous way, such as "rephrase it in English for dummies?"
10) Ask them to cut out the jargon
11) That went right over my head.

The things that constituted a friendship were friends talking with you, helping you out, having a laugh with you, providing a listening ear and a shoulder to cry on, and sharing things with you and you, them. Friends work as a team, offer constructive criticism where it's due, offer advice and suggestions, trust each other and, most importantly, they can just have quiet moments with each other when neither one has to talk, yet they are totally comfortable with this. Friends don't laugh at you when you are upset, backstab you, take advantage of your good nature, or concentrate on themselves all the time. They don't refuse to take you seriously or refuse to believe you. They don't think that your views are invalid, and they don't pressure you into doing things you don't want to do. I really could have done with this social skills group when I was younger, maybe then I wouldn't have stamped the word doormat on my greasy, acnefied forehead...If there is such a thing as battered friend syndrome (as opposed to battered wife syndrome) then I was it.

We also talked about different types of friends. There are three types: acquaintances, close friends or boy/girlfriends. We discussed how you would behave around each of the types. The teachers devised scenarios within friendships, from which the group had to say what was wrong and how we could respond differently. For example:

Julie: "I like your new haircut, it really suits you."

Shona: "Your hair could do with a cut actually. I bet you're jealous of my haircut. I
           could tell you what salon I went to."

The mistake here is that Julie would be hurt because Shona would feel insulted and might not have felt that there was anything wrong with her hair. Sometimes you have to be cruel to be kind, but what Shona said was unnecessary and uncalled for, even though it might be true in her mind. Asperger people are often characterised by their honesty, and honesty is good when it is needed, but sometimes it's better to push it aside where people's feelings are concerned. Through her honesty, Shona showed herself up to be either very childish, courageous or very stupid. She also seemed big-headed and maybe very insecure. Her reply made her sound like she wanted to boss Julie around and that's not friendship.

Julie could reply to the insult with something like "that's hurtful/uncalled for", "maybe it's your problem, not mine," or she could, although it's very improbable, thank Shona for being so truthful, although she would run the risk of only reinforcing Shona's behaviour. What would we have done differently? We all agreed that it was always best to thank someone for a compliment, and that we should not respond with a comment unless it is a positive one, i.e. "Thanks Julie - your hair looks great too".

We did other examples similar to that one and we also discussed things like: how to tell if someone likes you (they like you if they talk to you, smile at you, don't turn away, listen to you, give eye contact, stand near you, ask questions about you, involve you); when and how to start conversation; how we would clarify what the other person was saying; how we would keep the conversation going; when and how we would end a conversation; and how we would tell someone we wanted to be alone.

We always stressed the importance of thinking before you spoke and the unwritten rules of conversation. In a way, holding a conversation is like playing a card game, and there are ways of cheating that make it easier. Asperger people (well I can only really speak for myself) barely know the rules, but mainstreamers do, and they can cheat. If you don't know the rules then you can't play the game, let alone know how to cheat. It's hard to explain mainstreamers and their cheating business, but basically it's an opportunity thing where they can instantly latch on to something interesting and talk about it and there is no need for the formalities of conversation like "hello/how about you/nice shoes" etc. Imagine that two people are meeting in the street and suddenly a fabulous sports car goes zooming down the road, the duo then have the opportunity to cheat by talking about the sports car. I however have to go through the whole "hello/how about you/your family/cat/how was school/work/ college/uni/so did he phone you?" spiel, before I can talk about anything else. It's good for formal meetings, but my friends can find it a bit tedious. It's another one of my Asperger-induced routines.

Here is a collection of ideas from the group about when it might be difficult to start a conversation:
- When you don't agree with their principles - e.g. football, culture, race
- When you're angry or upset
- If you're shy
- With the opposite sex
- When entering another social group - e.g. at school or a party
- When it's a group of people you don't know
- When you're not adept at small talk
- When it's someone you've had an argument with
- When there is an obvious power scale - the other person has authority and you are the underdog, and it undermines your confidence
- When you are in a new place.

And what you might say to start a conversation:
- Say 'hello' and 'hey' genially
- Start with a compliment
- Ask them about themselves - their interests, hobbies. For example, if they're wearing a football shirt, maybe state the obvious and say "Oh, Linfield, my pal supports them, so he does"

- Use the weather as a last resort. Statements of fact might be boring but they can often launch a good conversation.

What you could say to keep a conversation going:
- "Tell me more..."
- Ask them how their life is and ask them for updates (only if you know them)
- Tell them about your day
- Mention current affairs - e.g. "A certain royal has foot and mouth disease - every time she opens her mouth she puts her foot in it!"
- "Have you heard the rumours?" (although gossiping is generally not good)
- Show interest in them
- Ask questions which begin with who, what, when, where, why and how
- Talk about things of mutual interest.

And how to end a conversation:
- "Sorry but I have to go now, can't stop to chat, I'll see you later"
- "Oh, I forgot/just remembered, I've got to go"
- "That's very interesting. I'll give it some thought"
- "Can I call you later?"

And how to tell someone we would like to be alone:
- "I think I'd like some time to myself (right) now"
- "I need to be on my own for a while"
- "Could you give me five minutes on my own, please?"

Prospects

Because of my inadequate workplace skills, I signed up for the Prospects course, which is a four week work training scheme, then a fortnight unpaid work placement. However, Prospects is different from any normal course because it's designed specifically for Asperger people. The package includes not only workplace instruction, but social skills training and motivational exercises designed to boost confidence. Hypothetically, students will leave the course with the basic necessary credentials to find a job which is, at least, realistic.
A problem shared by society in general, but most commonly Asperger people, is that we have a tendency to expect too much, especially with work. We want high powered jobs with £30K a year salaries, and we want them now, which is why so many of us are discontent in the workplace, or have given up looking for employment altogether.

It's a sad fact that many Asperger people have few or no qualifications (they're not all intellectually challenged - some are just too scared to go to school), so the hope of landing a mega-bucks job couldn't be more fantastical unless, of course, they are phenomenally talented in one area and just happen to strike it lucky. On the other hand, many Asperger individuals excel at school (despite the taunts), and go on to do the same at college and university. For those ones, that £30K+ salary can be so near and yet so far - they have got the intellectual capability to do the job but not, however, the social skills, although there are always exceptions. They are the ones who run their own businesses, or are quick to pick up on the social conduct of the workplace.

Prospects removes the veil from our eyes and helps us face reality. It also teaches us that money is not a means to an end. Happiness and fulfilment are. There is only so much that money can buy and, at the end of the day, a highly paid job is worth nothing if you don't enjoy it. Personally, I'd prefer to be in a £10-15K job I enjoyed rather than a £30K job I hated, despite the cash incentive. As long as it pays the rent, rates, and puts food on the table, a moderately-paid job suits me fine.

Induction

For the induction, my mother and I travelled to London to meet the Prospects manager, Anthony Lipski. Tony and his team made us feel very welcome and they were only too pleased to help. There was nothing condescending about their actions, which was refreshing. If there is one thing that really gets my goat it's being patronised because of my disability - I don't favour pity. The only person who is allowed to pity me is myself, end of story!

The sessions

Prospects is situated in Islington, North London, which meant I had to catch a few trains to get there. For the induction and the first two sessions, my mother travelled with me so she could be sure I knew the route. After that I had to get there on my own. Initially I was a bit nervous, because I was worried I might lose my way, but the journey became relatively simple once I'd got used to it. There were eight sessions in total, four of which were filmed under the careful scrutiny of the BBC cameras, for a documentary called *First Sight*. Yes, I was going to be made famous, if only for 15 minutes. I thought I could handle the course with the cameras and all that (as someone whose dream job would be an actress), but I found concentrating on what I was being taught, while also trying to perform for the cameras, pretty difficult. I shouldn't have even tried to perform at all, because they wanted to capture me as myself, not as some cheerful character I temporarily adopted.

There were two other clients with me - Dave (20) and Rose (28). As with the Social Skills Pilot Group, the difference between the three of us was remarkable. Dave was obsessed with World War Two and never shut up, Rose only spoke when she was spoken to. From the way he spoke and the things he said, it was clearly evident that Dave was far from mainstream, yet Rose couldn't be more different. She was highly articulate, intelligent, very straightforward and forthcoming. The only thing that highlighted her syndrome was her inability to initiate a conversation which, in fact, could have equally been nothing more than a contentment with her own company, rather than a developmental condition. Rose never said enough to annoy me, but I was constantly seeing red with Dave and, consequently, he with me. Penny, our teacher, played mediator, which was very helpful. Penny was informal but firm. She treated us as friends rather than pupils, but reinforced her authority in situations where Dave and I (Rose was a model pupil) weren't paying full attention. I have a problem with doodling. I doodle on every piece of doodle-able surface possible. I'm surprised Penny didn't clout me for the number of times I was scribbling on my worksheets instead of writing proper answers on them!

During the course, we learnt how to explain Asperger's syndrome to others, interview skills and how to adapt them, communication and socialisation skills, strategies for work and life, and (a basic but informative guide on) how to tackle stress. We discussed who we were and shared our personal experiences. We also compiled a list of what we thought Asperger's syndrome was and wasn't, what we wanted from the PDP (personal development program) course and a set of rules we should all adhere to.

Our rules:
1) To all co-operate with each other (me)
2) To respect each others opinions (Penny)
3) To listen to each other (Dave)
4) To work through challenges together (Rose)
5) To allow spontaneity and freedom of speech (me)
6) Not to interrupt each other talking (Rose)
7) Giving everyone a chance to talk (Dave)
8) To apologise if you're late (Rose)
9) To stay on the relevant subject (Dave)
10) Not to distract each other (Penny)

What we thought Asperger's syndrome was:
- By definition: a developmental disorder (me)
- A form of Autism (Rose)

- The reason why I went to a SLD (severe learning disability) school (Dave)
- Obsessions and rituals (Rose)
- Problems understanding others (Dave)
- The inability to relate to others (me)
- The reason why I'm writing a book (me)
- Not a sort of madness (very accurate point from Rose)
- The thing that labels me. I feel like I'm branded and that there is no alternative (me)
- Difficulty picking up on non-verbal signals (Rose)
- Difficulty knowing social rules and following them (Rose)
- Problems with social instinct (Rose)
- A spot or blot on the landscape. Something abstract in a concrete world - a variation (me)
- A hindrance where making friends is concerned (me).

From the above list and her suggestions, Penny got us to write our own explanation of Asperger's syndrome, as a preparation for how to explain it to others. Here is what I wrote:

> *Asperger's syndrome is a form of Autism that affects social and communicative skills. It is something that differentiates Aspees (Asperger's people) from mainstreamers. It is invisible and often only indicated by an odd walk or strange manner of speech. To some Aspees it is a hindrance but, to others, a gift or talent.*

> *Asperger's syndrome isn't a handicap, but it does disable me from knowing how to communicate with others in an acceptable way. Because it is on the Autistic spectrum people might assume that I'm mentally impaired, which is untrue. I'm more socially impaired, because it is difficult for me to relate to people. I depend on structure and control in order to conduct myself. It's not all negative though. I'm very single-minded and goal-orientated. I put all my effort into my work and always strive to do my best.*

Tackling interviews

For interviews, we were given invaluable tips that neither me nor Dave had ever considered. Penny fully informed us on the fundamentals of an interview and all the factors surrounding it, such as how we would travel to the interview, what we should wear, how we should behave and what we should already know about the role we're applying for. She advised us to plan our route to the interview and, if possible, practice that route at least once before to see how long it would take. Plan B was also important in case there were complications - such as trains running behind schedule, cars getting caught in traffic and buses running late. We were told to call the interviewer and tell them why we would be late.

Punctuality was crucial, so was politeness, a confident and positive demeanour and eye contact. Proactivity was encouraged - in that I mean asking (appropriate) questions as well as answering them. And so was an enthusiasm about ourselves and the job - no-one will hire you because they feel sorry for you (I used to think they would)! One-word answers were a big no no, so was fidgeting (I'm a compulsive hair-twiddler), mumbling, criticising previous employers and disagreeing with the interviewer. Honesty should be treated with caution. Say if we thought the interviewer's suit was dated, that sort of thing is better kept silent! I learnt that one from experience. In one interview the employer was wearing a dark green suit and I foolishly blurted out how I thought she looked like a cabbage (tact is a wonderful thing if you've got it, but it can be a death sentence if you havn't)!

Dress-wise, we had enough common sense to know to dress smartly and formally. Role-wise, Penny suggested we find out all we could about the employer, what our job role entailed and she stressed the importance of preparing a few questions of our own to pose to the interviewer - that way, we would be showing interest in the job, and would consequently have a better chance of landing our role.

Contrary to personal assumption, Penny told me to have no qualms about asking the interviewer to repeat or rephrase the question if I didn't understand it first time round. To get us into the mindset for proper interviews, we were filmed acting out this role-play situation over two sessions. We did a 'before' and 'after' take - comparing our first trial interview on the third session to our rehearsed, kitted-up one on the fourth session. Seeing ourselves on camera gave us the opportunity to criticise ourselves and to correct our faults. It was also a cringe-worthy experience, I can tell you! My first trial interview, after we were only briefed on a few interview techniques, was hideous! I giggled all the way through and acted a bit too informally for Pennys' liking. I seemed nervous, very immature and not at all clued up on the job. My second interview, however, went swimmingly. I toned down my accent - resulting in this obscure Lorraine Kelly sound-alike voice - sat up straight, smiled and acted like a professional. Apart from my cocky "See you Monday" departing line, I would have got the job.

The anxiety/catastrophe scale

This was a very straightforward and useful technique aimed at helping us keep things in perspective. We were shown a diagram of a ruler calibrated from 0 to 100. Major catastrophes, such as being diagnosed with a terminal illness, would be rated at 100, whereas minor accidents, such as spilling a glass of water on the carpet, would be around two. Redundancy and divorce ranked at around the 50 to 75 mark. With the anxiety scale, we were taught how to keep everyday things, such as missing the bus, in perspective so that our reactions to them wouldn't be up around the 90 mark and stress us out. I'm naturally a very highly-strung person (partly due to my bipolar affective disorder, which is explained in a later chapter) and I am provoked by the most trivial of things. Most of the time I'm able to deal with them, but on a particularly bad day I just let everything get to me and forgetting my pencil case can cast a shadow on the world. We were posed with a number of imaginary situations, upon which we had to rate our own reaction on the anxiety scale. I was very stressed that day anyway, which affected my mindset and, consequently, every given situation ended up on the 50 to 100 mark, when most of them should have been below it.

Penny discussed and reviewed our answers with us, correcting where we had gone wrong. She explained that the reason Rose and I had initially focused on the higher end of the scale could be because we had distorted thinking styles. I could only speak for myself, but I knew this was true. I was the reigning queen of filtering, catastrophising and blaming.

The term 'filtering' meant focusing on and magnifying the negatives in a situation until they outweighed the positives. Catastrophising meant expecting the worst, expecting not to cope well and then talking ourselves into it. Another form was exaggerating everyday events into the most dreadful of happenings. Blaming referred to us either holding other people and outside influences responsible for our unhappiness, or blaming ourselves for everything, telling ourselves we were hopeless and useless.

Once we realised this about ourselves, I felt able to reassess my scope on things. I know that I'm not a complete tragedy if my efforts fail. I realise that the Horsemen of the Apocalypse won't be knocking on my door if things aren't as I would like them. I acknowledge that I can't be liked by everyone, so I shouldn't blame myself entirely if I can't make friends in any given social situation. Likewise, I can't always be completely competent and fault-proof, so I shouldn't criticise myself for being less than perfect. If something is unpleasant or frightening, I know that worrying bucket loads about it won't do me any favours.

What we wanted from PDP

The aims Penny offered for us were much the same as the ones we offered for ourselves - developing a common understanding and personal explanation of our condition and to promote self-advocacy in explaining it to others; to explore vocational choices; to equipt us with an appropriate understanding of non-verbal communication; to realise the importance and effectiveness of social interaction through conversation; to be able to cope with team work; to build up our confidence, and to develop interview skills. These were realistic and achievable aims, so no-one seemed daunted by them.

What I wanted from PDP was to learn the necessary social skills to get along in the workplace; to gain further knowledge of, and insight into, my condition; to learn how to stop myself from stressing out over interviews; to learn how to communicate more fluently; and, finally, to improve my concentration span. I can honestly say there wasn't one aim left untouched. Penny altered the structure of the course around us and our wants and we all benefited from it. By the eighth session, Dave wasn't spouting forth about World War Two at every opportunity, I wasn't doodling as much, and Rose...? Well, there was no difference, but I don't think she needed to learn anything anyway! All throughout the course, we were encouraged to think positively about ourselves, and to focus on what talents we had, rather than the impairments.

What next?

After the PDP course, each client was to fulfil two weeks work experience, of which the first week was fully supported by a Prospects member of staff. Penny was going to support me. I was placed with the Radio Advertising Bureau for work experience, but unfortunately they moved to somewhere about two hours away, which prevented me from taking placement there. However, Penny scouted around for jobs that matched my criteria, and within a week had found me a placement at the Brentwood Theatre Company. I got on really well there, primarily because the environment was very easy-going and laid-back, with a considerable margin for the sort of social errors Asperger people make. What I mean by this is that, because it was a small company, with crazy, eccentric people like myself, my abnormal behaviour was tolerated. This was both a good and a bad thing.

Full marks go to Karen and co. at Brentwood theatre for being just pure magic and putting up with me. No marks go to me for my first week there when I failed to conduct myself as well as I should have. My problem is that whenever I get a chance to act recklessly I will. It's not that I don't think about the consequences, because I do, it's just that when I've got an impulse to do something I have to do it, and I can't emphasise this enough. Likewise when there's something I don't want to do, I used to refuse to do it. I am stubborn like that. I don't refuse to do things any more, because I realise doing things you'd rather not do is just what life's about, and if you don't accept that then you will get left behind. Like I said, the Brentwood Theatre was a lot less strict than your average place of employment, therefore it required more willpower for me to conduct myself in the proper work fashion.

Unfortunately, I took advantage of the situation (actually, come to think of it I probably didn't - I'm neither clever nor opportunistic nor manipulative enough to take advantage of any situation! So I'll say that anyhow, for want of a better phrase) and I took a few liberties. For example, I dawdled when running errands from place to place, absent-mindedly doodled in my notebook when I should have been making worthwhile notes, and pestered Karen for just one more cup of tea. Penny was not best pleased and I hate myself for disappointing her like that. I'm dubious as to whether any other employer would give me as many chances as Penny and Karen did, and I really shouldn't have abused their good nature by being such a tool.

In the second week, however, I caught myself on and just knuckled down to work. Penny hadn't been too pleased with my idle behaviour in the first week and had aimed a few cross words in my direction. Basically, I just had to pull my head out of the sand and face up to things. I have a habit of turning into an ostrich when I'm behaving in ways I shouldn't - hiding behind the guise that if I don't think about what I'm doing, then the fact that it's uncalled for will just go away, which is a really irresponsible way to behave for someone in any workplace, whether work for real or work experience.

Penny and Karen were pleased with my improvement in the second week, and I came away from my work experience with a really good feeling that I had accomplished something. I've been back to the Brentwood Theatre a few times because I really liked it there and I would certainly recommend it to any other Asperger person with or without a confidence problem. They made me feel relaxed and at home - maybe too much so - and they treated me just like any other employee. I didn't feel like I was being patronised because of my condition.

In my own experience, and through talking to other Asperger employees, I've learned that too many employers make the mistake of acting all condescending towards Autistic people, purely because Autistics fall under the disabled category. I know most of these employers are probably only trying to help, but I feel some of them just go too far. I might have learning difficulties and say and do inappropriate things at inappropriate times, but I didn't fall off the Christmas tree!

Another thing I learned about work experience was an important lesson for life. All the time I knew that even though this was only a practice, it was equally as important as the real thing, but in the beginning I tried to convince myself it wasn't, just so I could be the lazy, fat idle slob that I had been all my life. I knew my behaviour was out of order and that even though mainstreamers could carry it off flawlessly and probably get away with it, or if they didn't they could easily find another job, I couldn't. I've often felt that mainstreamers are allowed a much broader margin of error than people like myself and have been envious of their freedom and my confinement. Mainstreamers are so adept at social communication in comparison to me, they can get away with so much more. The weird introvert is persecuted for the slightest discrepancy, yet the bolshy streetwise mainstreamer can break the family heirloom and just shake it off.

The Brentwood Theatre Company, however, made me feel like that mainstreamer I was so desperate to be. They gave me the room mainstreamers have, allowing me to make those crucial mistakes and, with their directions, to learn from them. I've been scolded by many a person for being a complete idiot, but never given the opportunity to assess where and how I went wrong in the hope of correcting myself. Karen and Penny helped me learn and gain from my experiences. They opened doors for me that other people wouldn't, and started me on the road to eventually helping myself. I can honestly say my work experience with them was the most invaluable lesson I've ever learnt and the thing that makes me smile is I know they can do this for other Aspergers too.

The Hens

Another excellent opportunity arose from my time at the Brentwood Theatre. Karen was approached by three girls who had formed an acting group called The Hens (derived from their first initials - Hannah, Emily and Natalie), who wanted to act out a short play at the theatre. Because this play was only short they needed another longer play to do, and seeing as the play they were doing was about an Autistic girl, Karen told them about the play I had wrote and the rest, as they say, was history.

I met the girls and even though they deemed me a bit mental, they agreed to act out my play. I was ecstatic, so much so that for a few days I forget that I was a 12-stone ugly minger with a face like a pizza and hair like bog weed - and believe me that's saying something!
It was then I decided to prolong this autobiography so I could incorporate the Hens and their progress with my incredibly hard to comprehend play (really you'd need to be an acrobat to get your mind round it - it's insane to say the least, and very, very Asperger!). During this time I also devoted my attention to writing more mad plays and studying. If I had given every minute I spent on my studies or my other plays to this autobiography, the thing would be about 800 pages thick by now! But like a lot of Asperger people I am easily distracted. I get bored if I spend too much time on a singular thing. I find having four or five projects on rotation keeps me from getting bored, so everything takes eons longer to finish, but that's just a sacrifice I have to make. Quality takes precedence over speed, every time.

Here is a recent extract from my diary:

Penny says she's looking into getting me a Princes Trust grant, so I can set myself up properly as a scriptwriter and do all the necessary things that scriptwriters do; such as circulating the hype about my play and getting some publicity, producing decent flyers and travelling around to do some first-hand research for my characters. Nothing has happened yet, but I'm meeting up with Penny in three weeks to discuss plans and hopefully then something will have been sorted out. I shouldn't really be getting my hopes up, because it's unlikely I'd match the criteria for a Princes Trust grant anyhow, but what the hell! If it all goes pear-shaped then I hope there will be another avenue to explore, but we will have to cross that bridge when we come to it - or come to that bridge when we cross it, as my pal Emma used to say.

Hopefully by the time this book is published, I'll be well on the way to becoming a playwright superstar (aye Nita, catch yourself on!). Watch this space...

Outro

Brings a tear to the eye, just to say goodbye!

Well, as Bugs Bunny would say "that's all folks!" because you've reached the end of my book - unless you read books from back to front. So before you go, I demand to know where you're going, why, how, what you're doing and with whom. You don't have to tell me of course...You could just tell me how many pairs of socks you've got and why you're always wearing jodhpurs (Ah the tragedy! I was born at such an early age.) I'm wearing navy socks by the way, with a grey band across the top! Stick that on your chart of bizarre obsessions - because I was once obsessed with everything navy. That's about it folks! It is now safe to depart from the ride. Use the exit on your left and enjoy the rest of your day!

Eh? Where have you all gone?! Come back! Come back!!!

Nita stands outraged, bellowing down the microphone. The remainder of the nation is silenced. Tumbleweed sweeps its way over some far away land, where the echo reaches its final resound.

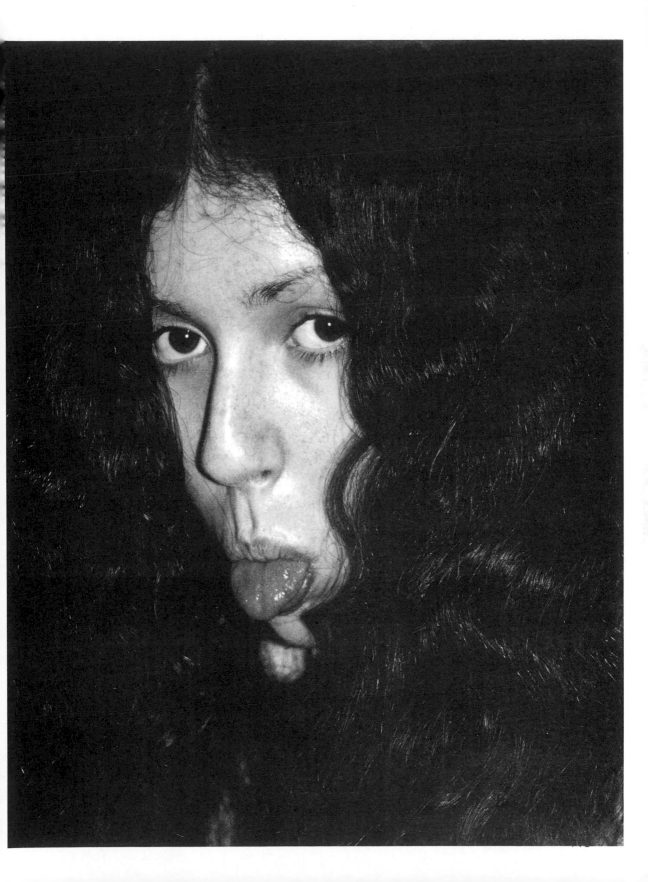

Appendix 1 - Other Voices
Back to Glesga!

In late February 2001, I returned to the land of rain, Rangers (and Celtic) and rowdiness, to interview a group of Asperger adults from the Strathclyde Autistic Society. Here, in it's full unedited glory, is my report. I am literally glowing with pride, oh yes, I am!

Mission statement

To acquire, through a questionnaire and face to face interviews, a wider perspective of how other Asperger individuals feel about having this condition and how they are coping with it, what they want out of life and how things could be improved for them.

Questionnaire

Chris and Harry (the two members who took part)

Names: Chris and Harry
Age: Chris (20) and Harry (19)

The following questions require more than a simple yes/no answer. You can write on the backs of the pages if there isn't enough space to fit your answers.

1) Do you work?
                (Chris) No
                (Harry) No
    a) If yes:
                Where?
                Did you find it easy/challenging to get the job?
                What were the reasons for this?
                Do you like it at your work? If so, why? If not, why not?
    b) If no:
                Do you have any other occupation (for example, voluntary work)?
                (Chris) I'm hoping to be doing painting and decorating soon.
                (Harry) I am part of the Dumbarton District Health Committee and
                several other groups.

2) Would you like to be in work? If so, why? If not, why not?

> (Chris) Yes, because it will get me out of the house and give me something to do.
>
> (Harry) No, I don't want to feel under pressure too soon.

3) Do you have a career plan or any ideas career-wise? Please explain them:

> (Chris) I plan to do voluntary work all my life.
>
> (Harry) No.

4) How long did it take to recognise that you were different? And at what age were you diagnosed?

> (Chris) I was diagnosed when I was four years old, but was about nine when I realised I was different.
>
> (Harry) Since about the age of eight, I felt more different than others. I was diagnosed at the age off 11.

5) Explain how you felt after you were diagnosed:

> (Chris) I didn't understand about Autism until I was 16.
>
> (Harry) Relieved to know that I had something to target. Disappointed to find out after I had left school.

6) Do you know of any family members who also have your condition? If so, please explain something about their personality. Is it very similar/different to yours? Do you relate to that person well?

> (Chris) No
>
> (Harry) No

7) Do you have any friends with the same condition? If so, please explain something about their personality. Is it very similar/different to yours? Do you relate to that person well?

> (Chris) I have a friend called Alex and we both have our favourite sayings. I relate to him very well.
>
> (Harry) I have many friends in the Asperger group and even though there are minor similarities (hard to make friends, low confidence) there is alot of difference.

8) How does your condition affect you in socialisation, communication and interaction with others?

> (Chris) I repeat sayings a lot and I find it annoying if people get on at me about it.

(Harry) Even though I try my best, I find it hard to socialise with some girls. If I'm bombarded with a set of verbal instructions, it takes me a while to fit it together.

9) Are you confident and outspoken, shy and silent, or in between? Do you know why you are like this?

(Chris) I'm in between. I am confident in conversations because I always have something to say, but I find it hard to stick up for myself in case the person reacts badly or says something I don't like.

(Harry) I put on a confident and outspoken front to help me improve my socialisation.

10) Do you suffer from mood swings, paranoia or anxiety? If yes, have you always been like this?

(Chris) I suffer from worry and I always have.

(Harry) Recently, if I feel under pressure too much, I have panic attacks.

11) Do you have a short temper? Do other people just generally annoy you?

(Chris) I do have quite a short temper when things annoy me.

(Harry) Yes, if someone gets on my nerves, it is very hard to shake off, even though it works sometimes.

12) Are you easily excitable and enthusiastic?

(Chris) Yes.

(Harry) Yes.

13) Do you think you have a sense of humour?

(Chris) I do have a sense of humour sometimes. It depends on what mood I'm in.

(Harry) Yes

14) Generally, are you an optimist, pessimist or in between? Why?

(Chris) I'm in between. It depends on what mood I'm in.

(Harry) Optimist - things can only get better if you try hard enough to look on the positive side.

15) Would you like to have more friends?

> (Chris) I think more friends would be nice, but I've got quite
> a lot of friends.
> (Harry) Yes

16) What was school like for you? What sort of experience did you have - good or bad?

> (Chris) I liked school when I was younger, but as I got older I hated
> it because the staff were telling me what to do a lot.
> (Harry) School was so far the worst part of my life so far (especially
> secondary school). I acted very immaturely at first, which led to me
> being bullied. On top of all that, I had a crush on a girl and it all
> landed on top of me. In the fifth year I had a nervous breakdown.

17) Is there anything else about you that you think I should know? Do you have any
further comments?

> (Chris) Not really.
> (Harry) No

Thanks for your co-operation,
Nita

Meeting the group

I didn't get to choose who I interviewed - it was all a matter of who was available and who was willing to be interviewed. If I had my choice I would have interviewed two girls and two boys, to get a fair idea of the experience of both sexes. Unfortunately, only three members were available that day. Initially I was upset because I thought I wouldn't get nearly enough information, but when I met these three I was pleasantly surprised. I got to interview Chris (20), Harry (19) and Peter (23), all very amicable characters, each with a vibrant, individual personality and mountains of stuff to say. I left with a wealth of info that I planned to painstakingly sift through for hours to extrapolate the most notable bits. That was going to be tough, because all of it was relevant, but that's the nature of interviews - keep everything and this book would be over the designated word limit and submittance deadline!

However, disaster struck. Only the first 20 minutes of the interview was audible. I don't know the reason why (maybe I wasn't holding the mic close enough - I know I pressed record when I was supposed to), but the other 70 minutes didn't come out at all, it was as if the tape was blank. Naturally, I was very upset, because I had to go by memory rather than audible evidence. That meant I had to summarise and I hate summarising people who have such depth.

Here are the best bits from the first 20 minutes of my interview with Chris:

Me: So Chris, tell me a bit about yourself and the group.

Chris: I've been a member of the group since 21st April 1998. I enjoy it here. We do a wide variety of things like playing sports like pool or badminton. We play board games, have a barn supper once a year, we go ten pin bowling, and on the first Sunday of every month we go on walking groups around the West of Scotland. I think probably my favourite activity in the group is going out for a meal. We sometimes do that. One time we went to an Italian cafe and then another time we went to the Counting House. It used to be a bank but now it's a pub. I think that's how it's called the Counting House.
I've stayed in Glasgow all my life and sometimes I think I might prefer to be in the countryside. Maybe I want a change of scenery...Generally I think the country is nicer - fewer people.

Me: Does the hustle and bustle of the town confuse you, then? All the sounds, colours, all that stimuli? Does it get to you like it does me?

Chris: No, I don't get that at all.

Me: That's fortunate. I thought it was a general Asperger thing, but obviously it's not. What sort of problems do you think you have when you're out in the town doing your shopping? Any sort of problems - general, specific, anything?

Chris: Well, I don't really have a problem with going shopping or going up the town. I'd have difficulties if I didn't write it down in a list. I write a long list and check it every few minutes.

Me: Apart from shopping, do you go up the town often?

Chris: When I go into town it's usually for a McDonalds or something. I don't go clubbing or anything. I used to go to a roleplay club, but the game was vastly complicated and quite demanding so I stopped.

Me: Have you got many pals here?

Chris: I have a few pals, yeah. In the group I have some pals. There's a guy who used to go to my school who goes to the group. There used to be a guy who I would tag along with when he went out places.

Me: It's good that you're popular, because a lot of Asperger people have few or no friends at all. I've got pals now, but mostly everyone hated me in the past.

Chris: Why is that?

Me: They thought I was weird and a lot of them found it hard to get along with me. OK, the inevitable question: has anyone ever started on you because of your disability? They have started on me many a time.

Chris: I don't think anyone's tried to beat me up or anything. I suppose part of my Autism is that I repeat certain phrases and at school I think the other kids tried to hurt me, because you know what it's like when people are annoying you and then you're intent on hurting them? Well they used to pick on me but it was always with words. This guy made fun of me because I cricked my head like a chicken. But the lecturer at college gave him a row and anyway I didn't really care because the guy was just an ignorant wee git. He never did any work and just messed about. He was very disruptive.

Me: In the questionnaire you said that you don't have a job, but that you do volunteer work. What sort of volunteer work do you do?

Chris: What I'm hoping to do is painting and decorating. I'm working at a charity shop the now because I really like working for a charitable cause. I've worked in charity shops in the past and I've also done some conservation work. You don't get paid, but I think that's better because if I did get paid my benefits would be cancelled. And anyway, even if I did get a good job there would be no guarantee it would last. I have to be realistic about these things. At least I know where I am with volunteer work and I can always stop if I need a wee rest. There's no pressure.
I'm on benefit and I'll be on benefit the rest of my life, but that's right for me. I care about money - I think what it is is that I'm just being sensible about it. I'm staying on benefits because it's a safer option than getting a job, when there's no guarantee a job would last. I mean if I got a good job and my benefits got cancelled, but then the job didn't last, then what?

Me: Have you got a girlfriend?

Chris: Well there is this girl I've sort of been fancying at college, at the social skills evening class. She fancies me - I mean there's every sign of it.

Me: Is she Autistic?

Chris: No she's not.

Me: How did you react when you found out you had Asperger's Syndrome?

Chris: I'm not sure. I was diagnosed as Autistic when I was four but I ignored it until I was sixteen when I knew for sure I had Autism. When I was a wee boy my mum told me I was Autistic and she was talking about Autistic children. I thought it was my fault that I had Autism, why I was doing these things. I didn't like it so I ignored the fact that I had Autism and refaced it when I was sixteen. I always knew there was something different about me, but I didn't know what. Being different upset me. My stepmum was always getting on at me about social skills, whereas other people in my family let me get away with things. Me stepmum said I learnt my social skills a bit later, whereas other people would had already learnt them by then. When I was sixteen and I knew I had Autism, I was angry because it was this which prevented me from developing social skills.

Me: Do you think you've got enough social skills now or do you think you could learn some more?

Chris: I think you can always improve on social skills. But I'm a nice enough guy, I'm popular enough, so I guess I've learnt some. Although I could do with learning a few more. I need to understand the words people use better. Because of my Autism, I can't really understand the words, so I try to blank things out or change the story in my head.

Me: Do you think that you did well at school academically?

Chris: I did the work OK, but I didn't really get along with the staff.

Harry

Like I said, after 20 minutes the tape blanked out, so I didn't even get a snippet of either interview with Harry or Peter. I have a poor memory, but I racked my brain for all it was worth and wrote down what I could.

Harry is 19, very confident and jovial. He is so direct and socially intact that I couldn't believe he has a developmental disorder at all. In my opinion, he's a mainstreamer. Maybe Asperger's Syndrome was a mis-diagnosis? He could very possibly have bipolar disorder (see next chapter), but possibly bipolar II rather than the classic bipolar 1. But absolutely nothing about him was indicative of Asperger's Syndrome. He answered every question directly, was excellent with jokes, perfect with eye contact, never repeated himself or stammered. His social skills couldn't be faulted, his writing is neat and legible, his walk portrays no odd gait, he has no spasms or bizarre tics or twitches. His sister doesn't believe he has Asperger's Syndrome either. She says he's acting to get attention. The acting it I can believe, but the attention-seeking I can't. Harry doesn't come across as that type. He's been through a lot - suicide attempts, brief hospitalisation (because he was a danger to himself), depression and a nervous breakdown.

These were due to him not feeling accepted in society and because he was rejected by a girl he really cared about. I don't blame him. When I was rejected by a boy I really cared about, I was distraught for absolutely ages. Like Harry, I thought this person cared about me as much as I did about them, but it turned out I was just being ridiculed behind my back. But isn't that just a common problem for everyone, not specifically Asperger people?

Despite all these problems, Harry presented himself in a really confident and straightforward manner. He said the confidence was all an act and that underneath it all he was just as insecure as anyone. I can believe that, because sometimes I have to act confident when inside I'm the most insecure person you could ever meet. But Harry's seems to be a more natural, plausible confidence than mine. Harry knows how to moderate his emotions, whereas I just go completely full throttle forward like Schumacher at the Grand Prix - too confident, too boisterous, too much of a loud-mouth. Maybe I should look up the word restraint and take some tips from it!

Peter

The third person I interviewed was Peter. Peter was 23 years old, softly spoken and friendly, He had a lot to say and, like the other two, had his head screwed on. He might have been a touch shy, but he seemed to overcome it. His Asperger's syndrome was noticeable, but not until I got into a conversation with him, and even then you could have put his difference down to good old fashioned shyness and politeness.

I have the worst memory, so I can't recall much of what he said in his interview. However, what I do remember is that he had this remarkably insightful view into people's characters (rare in Asperger people), repeated a specific phrase time and time again, and was very content in himself about who he was and the condition he was affected by. We discussed school and the inevitable topics of bullying, alienation and depression, but I honestly can't remember what he said. I think he had experienced some trouble, but if he had, then either he was well over it or it didn't bother him. He didn't appear scarred or weakened by his troubles like some other Asperger people I know. Peter had been in a relationship with an older woman, proving that Asperger people aren't destined to be celibate, which we discussed. They had sustained the relationship for a long time, but eventually Peter had ended it because the woman was taking his affections for granted. If there was one thing I remember about Peter, it was that he had common sense, which many Asperger people lack. Peter didn't let himself get abused and strung along by his girlfriend like I did with my so-called friends. He was courageous enough to take a stand, which is something that's taken me all my life to learn.

I would have liked to speak more to Peter, but he had a deadline, so I didn't get to ask him all that I planned to.

Conclusions

Both Chris, Harry and Peter were great people to meet. All of them had been through difficult times but, had persevered with their lives which I think is commendable, rather than becoming a social recluse like me. I've kept in contact with Harry and am going back to Glasgow to see him soon.

Overall I returned from the trip enlightened, knowing a lot more about my condition and how differently it can affect people. I really enjoyed the interviewing and hope to do it again sometime. I submitted a request to the *Asperger United* publication, asking for any Asperger people aged 12+ who would like to participate in my interviews. Unfortunately, no-one replied. Maybe I'll try again later or maybe I'll just forget about it. At the time of writing, my life has just sunk down the toilet in every way possible, and I'm not optimistic about anything, so that's the reason for all the indecision.

Special thanks to Andy Horseman who runs the group, for organising the interviews.

Appendix Two
Associated Syndromes

Irlen's Syndrome

The following description of Irlen's Syndrome has been copied from the internet. I could say this was because I couldn't write a more comprehensive description myself but that's not true. The truth is that at the time of writing, copying even, I was very depressed and my brain just wasn't working. I didn't have writers block. I just couldn't be bothered to do anything but sit in my room munching through twenty packets of crisps and cry.

Scotopic Sensitivity Syndrome and the Irlen Lens System

Written by Stephen M. Edelson, Ph.D., Center for the Study of Autism, Salem, Oregon

> *"There is growing evidence, based on both research and personal reports, that many autistic individuals see their world in a maladaptive, dysfunctional manner. Researchers at U.C.L.A. and the University of Utah have found evidence of abnormal retinal activity in autistic individuals. Additionally, there are many visual problems which are often associated with autism, such as reliance on peripheral vision; tunnel vision; hypersensitivity to light; and stereotypic (repetitive) behaviour near the eyes, such as hand-flapping and finger-flicking. Donna Williams, an autistic adult, has written several books about her life and has often commented on her vision. She once wrote: "Nothing was whole except the colours and sparkles in the air..." and "I had always known that the world was fragmented. My mother was a smell and a texture, my father a tone and my older brother was something which moved about."*

Scotopic Sensitivity/Irlen Syndrome is a visual-perceptual problem which occurs in some people with learning/reading disorders, autism and other developmental disorders. People with Scotopic Sensitivity/Irlen Syndrome experience 'perceptual stress' which can lead to a variety of perceptual distortions when reading and/or viewing their environment. Scotopic Sensitivity is triggered by one or more components of light, such as the source of the light (fluorescent lighting, sun), luminance (reflection, glare), intensity (brightness), wavelength (colour), and/or colour contrast.

As a result, the person may experience:

- Light sensitivity - bothered by brightness, glare, types of lighting
- Inefficient reading - letters on page move, dance, vibrate, jiggle
- Inadequate background accommodation - difficulty with high contrast
- Restricted span of recognition - tunnel vision or difficulty reading groups of letters
- Lack of sustained attention - difficulty maintaining attention

The Irlen Lens System, developed by Helen Irlen, was designed to treat Scotopic Sensitivity/ Irlen Syndrome. Helen Irlen has developed two methods to treat Scotopic Sensitivity: firstly, the use of coloured transparencies or overlays to improve reading; and secondly, tinted glasses to improve one's visual perception of his/her environment.

Transparencies

Transparencies or overlays are used to reduce perceptual stress while reading. For some people, letters/words on a page are not perceived clearly and/or not perceived in a stable manner, i.e. letters and words appear to move. The white background may overtake and dominate the person's perceptual system and the black print of the text may fade into the background. Other symptoms may include having difficulty reading for relatively long periods of time, developing headaches and feeling dizzy. It is possible that, for some, the high contrast between black print on a white background provides excessive stimulation to the visual system and thus interferes with the reading process. In the Irlen Lens System, coloured transparencies are placed over printed text with the result that these problems may be reduced or eliminated. A coloured overlay, such as a light blue transparency, placed over the text, will reduce the contrast between black and white as well as reduce the dominance of the white background. The optimal colour of the transparency required depends upon each person's unique visual-perceptual system.

Glasses

In addition to reading problems, people with Scotopic Sensitivity/Irlen Syndrome may have difficulty perceiving their surroundings. Many autistic individuals wear tinted glasses, which were prescribed by Helen Irlen or at one of her 76 worldwide diagnostic clinics, and have reported rather remarkable benefits. After wearing her glasses, Donna Williams wrote:

> *"These [Irlen] glasses would have changed all that. Faces and body parts and voices would have been whole and understood within a context of equally conjoined surroundings."*

Other autistic individuals report seeing better, feeling more relaxed, being less bothered by sunlight and/or indoor lighting, and having fewer perceptual distortions which can affect small and gross motor co-ordination.

Helen Irlen has developed effective methods for determining if a person suffers from Scotopic Sensitivity/Irlen Syndrome. She has also designed a standardised set of procedures which can determine the correct colour prescription for the transparency and the tinted lenses most sutable for each person.

(taken from http://www.autism.org/irlen.html)

Mom/Teacher

This response was submitted by J.K. Moore on 2/21/97.

"With 20+ years of teaching and 20+ years of parenting, I thought that I had seen or heard of all varieties of learning disabilities/dysfunctions. When my 16 year old daughter continued to have migraines that were unexplainable, I insisted on dyslexia screening. Since she was ranked 47 in a class of 597 at a well-known academic suburban high school, my request was met with less than enthusiasm. The testing revealed nothing of significance. All scores were in the 90% range except visual perception, which was in the 70% range. She was dismissed as not having a problem. During a discussion with a friend in a teacher's lounge of a school that I visit regularly in my job, I mentioned my daughter's migraines. A woman sitting next to my friend said that she had received some information that sounded like my daughter and would send it to me. Several days later I received what I now consider to be a lifeline for my daughter. The information was on Irlen's Syndrome or Scotopic Sensitivity Syndrome. After researching on the Internet, I contacted the Irlen Institute and found a SSS diagnostician about 20 miles from our home. During testing over the Christmas holidays, my daughter was diagnosed with SSS. As a parent, I have seen my daughter have some happy experiences, but none have been as wonderful as her face after using the filter for one day. She said that it was so easy to read. Two days ago she received her lenses and two hours later (thank goodness for one hour optical shops) she was wearing them. She loves what she sees. She no longer gets headaches from reading. She had never known that the rivers and light/dark print was not what

everyone else saw. She thought that she was seeing the same as everyone else. Now she knows what she has missed and is determined not to miss anything else.

As a parent and a teacher, I know that it is real. Some children labelled incorrectly have gone through years of school with mild to moderate problems that are completely treatable. I have no doubt that my daughter and others like her will benefit from the filters and lenses. I will carry the guilt with me for years that I did not find the reason for her migraines sooner. To help others with this problem has become my 'mission' and I tell 'Lyndsey's story' to anyone who will listen."

(taken from http://med-aapos.bu.edu/publicinfo/store2/Mom.Teacher3.25PM.html)

How it's related to Asperger's syndrome

I can't answer this, but my friend Anne Pemberton has a son who has both Asperger's Syndrome and Irlen's Syndrome. The excellent writer Donna Williams was also an Irlen patient and the two syndromes are often connected to each other (according to textbooks). I felt that it was important to include a section about Irlen's Syndrome, as I suspect that I might have it and that a lot of intelligent Asperger people also have it and don't know. As we all know, Asperger syndrome and other syndromes aren't mutually exclusive. Dyspraxia, dyslexia, bipolar disorder and obsessive compulsive disorder are common in the Autistic field and so, if some of us also have Irlen's Syndrome, then I can't afford to be complacent about it.

Bipolar Affective Disorder

Bipolar affective disorder is not abbreviated to BAD as you might expect, because it is no laughing matter. Formerly known as manic depression, it affects about 1% of the population in the UK (and over 1.2% in the US). Research strongly suggests that it is a hereditary mental illness, related to an instability in the transmission of the brains' nerve impulses. In plain English, it's a biochemical problem - a chemical imbalance in the brain.

Consequently, people with bipolar disorder are acutely vulnerable to emotional and physical stress and suffer greatly from its varying repercussions. Some can't sleep, others sleep too much; some lose their appetite, others overeat; some get aggressive and angry, others become weak and tearful. As with any illness, there are degrees of severity and how it affects bipolar disorder sufferers (I'm using the term 'suffering' in the literal sense) depends on the individual and the type of bipolar disorder they have (I'll explain these types later on).

For me, bipolar disorder began at age 12, although there is no set age for it to start. It most commonly surfaces in adolescence or early adulthood, but sometimes it begins in early childhood or doesn't arise until middle age. Going back to the first paragraph, bipolar disorder is thought to be hereditary, as some say Autism is (it is important to note that unlike the opposing view on the cause of Autism, you can't blame bipolar disorder on the MMR triple jab). My second cousin is a manic depressive and her son is Autistic. I've recognised depressive traits in my aunt and Autistic ones in my parents. However, none of them have any formal diagnosis.

Bipolar disorder is not, to my knowledge, invariably linked with Autism or Asperger syndrome. It is associated with it in several cases (I know two other Asperger individuals with bipolar disorder), but is not the route of the problem. Some Asperger people get depressed, some get that extra bit depressed, some get extremely depressed and some inherit bipolar disorder - the difference is subtle, but there is a difference. The human personality has a range of emotions and everyone suffers from mood swings from time to time. They wouldn't be human if they didn't. Emotions are neurological phases. The distinction between a mere neurological phase and bipolar disorder is that with bipolar disorder your moods are not generally dictated by, or related to, your situation. Situational depression - if you lose your job, or a loved one dies - is easy to relate to. The bipolar sort of depression, however, is dictated by the bipolar disorder. It controls you, unless you take medication to stabilise it. You can be having the most perfect day, happy days for bipolar disorder sufferers are called hypomanic episodes - when suddenly depression creeps up and hits you right in the face, and no matter how happy you were a minute ago, you just sink into this huge dank cavern of depression which you can't do anything about. Your mood swing swerves vastly out of proportion and, with it, your whole world does too. The former happy hypomanic episode and the latter major depression episode are no mere mood swings, they are what is known as bipolar phases.

Phases

Bipolar disorder is characterised by cyclical phases (note: this is my own personal explanation, not a clinical one, so most of it is coloured by my Asperger's Syndrome. I describe the phases as I experience them, so don't worry if a clinical definition is what you want and my description doesn't sound all that clinical:

1) Mania (euphoric mania and dysphoric mania)
2) Hypomania (can also be euphoric or dysphoric)
3) Depression
4) Mixed states (usually combined with suicide impulses)

1) Mania

My first stage of euphoric mania often begins with a warm, contended feeling. I look in the mirror and I think "OK, maybe I'm not so fat and hideous" and I smile a lot. At this time I find myself becoming more creative (much of this book was written under the influence of mania - both euphoric and dysphoric) and I want to go out and party! I'm happy, but I don't know why. Then the feeling escalates and BOOM, I'm giggling all the time and getting excited over absolutely nothing. I'm more active and productive and you will be hard pressed to get a word in edgeways because I never stop talking! My thoughts race and when talking I leap from subject to subject in a matter of minutes. The distraction level is high at the time of writing - I'm working on a further four books, because my attention never settles on anything for more than 10 minutes.

My usual bedtime is around 6am, but I'm out of bed by 11, going berserk dancing to my CDs, although I still end up gaining profound amounts of weight (probably in relation to my underactive thyroid gland). At this time I'm also very liable to be reckless and stupid, but I don't realise this because I'm blinded by an inflated ego. I'll go out and spend the little money I have on things that I know won't last, and sometimes, I even run into debt. However, the period of euphoric mania can be followed by a prolonged bout of dysphoric mania (note that periods of dysphoria can similarly occur in the hypomania and depression phases as well - and with me, they invariably do).

Dysphoria is when my high takes on a different guise, like an actor playing a part. It's still a high, just a different type. I become unusually irritable, impatient, stressed, paranoid to the extent where I won't leave the house, cranky due to insomnia, and everyone irritates me (which usually results in blazing rows over nothing at all). I'm adamant that I am right and everyone else is wrong. Any slight change in routine or order is immediately a red alert. Actually, slightly psychotic seems like a more appropriate term for me at this stage! I get increasingly agitated over trivial things and get panic-stricken too. I'm very impulsive too. I rip up sheets and T-shirts on a whim, I throw money away on stuff I don't need. I even tried to jump out my bedroom window on the spur of the moment once. On a few occasions I suffered bizarre hallucinations and was severely delusional. The 'whitecoats' prescribed me Haleperidol and I was practically comatose for the week I was on it.

2) Hypomania

In plain English, hypomania literally means a milder form of mania. The symptoms are similar to mania, but less severe, and they don't interfere so much with how I run my life. Whereas with mania, all the rational, sensible parts of my brain have swanned off to the Caribbean, hypomania impairs me much less and I feel more in control. If I'm living in an elevated state of euphoria, I have confidence in myself and am just as productive as with mania, the exception being I can concentrate better. I'm not as restless, but sometimes this is an incredibly subtle difference, which is why it's hard to tell. If I'm experiencing dysphoric hypomania, I'm irritable, tempestuous and argumentative, just not as severely. I still want to socialise, but find that I get agitated by most people and end up saying something I shouldn't and getting a black eye for it! Sometimes, however, it is difficult for me to draw a distinction between my manic episodes and hypomanic episodes, because the two are so closely associated. The only criteria for which I can make a subjective assessment is whether I am delusional or not. Of course, I can never tell if I'm delusional, I just have to go by what other people tell me. Apparently, I'm totally unreasonable and unreachable in my manic episodes, but in my hypomanic ones I'm relatively level-headed (as level-headed as an Asperger teenager can get).

Hypomania can go in two directions, it either escalates to full-blown mania or crashes to depression. I stopped taking my medication once during hypomania and descended into depression's murky depths for weeks. Unfortunately, I've always been geared towards the pessimistic side of things and am more likely to get depressed rather than manic.

3) Depression

As I mentioned before, depression is usually the sequel to dysphoric hypomania. The difference between the two is that with depression, I'm not sociable or creative (apart from one exception - my diary, which is my closest confidant) and I certainly don't try to be funny. During a major depressive episode, I really just want to curl up in my bed and stay there for all eternity. I cry for no reason. I avoid social contact because I have neither the energy nor want to be with people. This is not me being selfish, it's a part of my illness.

My interest in activities plummets quickly and because of this I feel useless and pathetic. I'm not likely to hit out, as with dysphoric mania, but rather withdraw into myself and become the timid little doormouse - fat on scraps of food but nevertheless easily stepped upon and crushed. I can't think either, because my mind is literally dead (along with my concentration and memory), filled with an all-pervasive attitude that I am living under a permanent rain cloud.

I gain a terrible amount of weight, because I often seek solace in food, but I taste nothing. I try exercising the calories off, but am just too exhausted to get past first base. My whole existence plays through slow motion, I move slowly, talk slowly and don't have the energy to think that much. However, there is one thought that constantly plagues my mind and that's the contemplation of suicide (although I care about my family and friends too much to actually go through with it, despite how much I'd like to). I look in the mirror and see a huge fat walrus of a girl, puffy, bloated face, double chin, body like the Michelin man merged with a sumo wrestler and I just want to die. No-one understands. All the people I know are too polite to be honest with me about my rapidly-escalating weight and I hate them for it. Everything is hopeless and I sink into a pit of despair. I feel empty, despite having eaten three huge tubs of bio yoghurt and a whole packet of cereal, consumed by an overpowering sense of sorrow and loss. The world is shrouded by fog. I develop psychosomatic illnesses and harshly recriminate myself for being so stupid ("What right do I have to make myself ill? I'm too fat and grotesque to deserve that!" Kind of a contradiction, considering I don't feel I have the right to be perfectly well either). Self-contradictory, indecisive, disorganised...I deserve nothing. I have a right to nothing.

4) Mixed Episode

This phase is truly a nightmare. The cycle doesn't necessarily result in a mixed episode, but when it does it's the most debilitating thing ever. In my case, a mixed episode involves either a simultaneous combination of dysphoric mania (never, never euphoric) and depression, or the frequent alternation of the two. It is horrible. I'm restless, riddled with anxiety and agitation, completely panic-stricken and feel desperately helpless. At the same time I have no confidence, no hope and look as forlorn as a lost puppy. I can be exhausted and silent one minute then loud and hyperactive the next. Expect tears, lots of them. Expect smashed crockery and torn-up cushions. Expect sweat, from all the kicking and running about. Expect blood, from cutting myself. Expect burns, from holding my hands over cigarette lighters and stubbing cigarettes out on my skin.

I'm extremely vulnerable to suicidal impulses during a mixed episode. I get to the point where I'm holding that razor at my wrists and the temptation to cut is overwhelming...but something stops me: the love for my family and friends. As long as they're alive and with me then I'll never be able to kill myself. That's good in a sense, because without them I wouldn't have been here to write this book, but it's also very disheartening.

How, you ask, can love and friendship be disheartening? Well sometimes, when you really want to end it all, having people who care for you sort of ruins your chances of escape, doesn't it? Sometimes I just wish they would all hate me, really really hate me, so I could finish it. I want to end it but I can't because of all the mess and devastation I'd leave behind, and that just exacerbates things.

Rapid Cycling Bipolar Disorder;

With me, the cycle of mania, hypomania, depression, mixed repeats itself usually within a matter of weeks and sometimes even days. This is because I have a less common form of bipolar disorder known as rapid cycling. This basically means that I go through the four phases at least once a year instead of the average four episodes over a decade. It's like a rollercoaster, a very tall, very frightening one. It might be my Asperger's syndrome that causes it, but then again it might not. I don't know if the two are even intertwined in that way. I'm not permanently cycling though, although I'm never normal either. There are intermittent times when it's just me and my Asperger's syndrome having a tea party with our friend Miss Underactive Thyroid and her pals Miss Dyspraxia and Miss Tinnitus, but Miss Rapid Cycling Bipolar Disorder isn't invited. But I'm never normal. Never. I wouldn't know normal if it hit me in the face.

Strangely enough, research proves that most rapid cyclers are female, have thyroid problems, didn't see eye to eye with lithium, and have taken antidepressants - my story exactly. It suggests no link to Autism though.

Some people develop rapid cycling because of overdosing on antidepressants (called chasing) in the hope of triggering a hypomanic episode or a high. A bipolar Asperger friend of mine went through a period of taking three times the recommended dose of Prozac. Yes, she got happy, unnervingly happy, for a while. Then the inevitable crash occurred and she became more depressed than ever. Fortunately, my friend didn't develop rapid cycling, but a small percentage of bipolar sufferers do.

Rapid cycling can also result from not having treatment (which is probably one of the reasons I've got it). The bad news about rapid cycling is that it gets worse as the years go by (apparently). But I'm willing to accept that, unless the scientists come up with some miracle treatment.

Bipolar I Disorder

Known as the classic form of bipolar disorder, this pattern is clinically defined as depression plus mania or mixed states. It involves enduring periods of mania or mixed episodes followed by equally enduring periods of depression. People who were ill initially with a manic episode are considered to have bipolar I disorder and will most probably have accompanying depressive episodes in the future unless they get treatment.

Bipolar II Disorder

More common than rapid cycling, but less common than bipolar I disorder, this patterns clinical definition is depression plus hypomania. The person suffers the full extent of the depression, but never a full-blown manic episode. Hypomania is where it stops. The absence of mania is what makes bipolar II disorder more difficult to recognise. Without mania, the undiagnosed person might not realise they have bipolar disorder at all. Bipolar II disorder sufferers can often overlook treatment for hypomania, concentrating instead on just the depression. But be cautious of taking only antidepressants, because they carry the risk of inciting a high (which will inevitably result in a crash), and/or more frequent cycles.

I'm not a doctor and I don't know as much about this pattern as I do my own, so I can't really offer any advice on medication here. However, as you probably know there is a wealth of information on the internet, the best of it (in my opinion) on the sites I've listed under the section on medication, (page 134).

Schizo-Affective Disorder

This term describes not so much a pattern of bipolar disorder as an overlapping condition. It has more to do with the psychotic symptoms than actual phases or moods. Manic and/or depressive episodes are accompanied by persistent delusions and hallucinations, and so are periods of normality, when the mood symptoms are not present. With bipolar disorder, any psychotic symptoms end when those particularly severe manic and/or depressive periods fade away. With schizo-affective disorder they are more stubborn.

The textbook tells me that bipolar disorder can be treated, but if it's not, some people can still make full recovery between episodes and symptoms don't re-occur for years. Others, however, might continue to suffer episodes to a lesser extent or be constantly depressed. I don't entirely understand why the symptoms would get milder without treatment, because it's the opposite with rapid cycling. Maybe that just highlights how different the bipolar patterns are?

Medication

Bipolar disorder is a life long illness and no amount of medication can make it go away. Drugging you up to the eyeballs solves nothing, yet the absence of preventative medication can be fatal. I've been on medication for a long long time, and have clocked up a list of prescription drugs the length of my arm, Prozac, Lithium, Lustral, Haleperidol, Zoloft... Currently, however, I'm only taking Prozac, because I've become medication-phobic. I have also felt sorely disappointed with previous medications, because none of them seemed to help. I know I should be on mood stabilisers but, for the life of me, I'm too terrified of them to make an appointment with my GP. A lot of them have very unsavoury side-effects too, the most off-putting in my opinion being weight gain (I'm already overweight, despite being on Thyroxine - maybe the Prozac interferes with it?).

Medication is a long and complicated subject, and I regret that this book has a deadline, because it gives me an excuse to be a lazy arse and completely forgo the whole section on medication. I've researched the subject on the internet, and found a number of clear, informative sites that will tell you everything you need to know (including recommended reads, support groups and associations):

> http://www.psychguides.com/bphe.html
> http://www.moodswing.org/faq.html
> http://cspo.queensu.ca/~anglesio/faq
> http://home.att.net/~mercurial-mind
> http://www.have-a-heart.com/bipolar-depression.html

The other view

The other school of thought is that bipolar disorder is not a chemical imbalance, but some kind of spiritual awakening, such as psychic vampirism or something like that. I like to think I'm broad-minded, so I can kind of relate to this alternative possibility. Am I learning the mystical powers of other-worldly energies such as chi, prana or kundalini? I'm not really clued up on all this mystical stuff. I'm trying to make up my own mind, but it's hard when the doctors are telling me that all this spiritual stuff is crap and the spiritualists are telling me the doctors are also talking toilet material. Right now I think I'll just stick with what I know - what the doctors tell me. When I'm in the grip of an episode I can't deny that it's powerful, and that if the emotion was there to be channelled into some spiritual force it would make sense. It honestly does feel like some sort of power is fighting to break free, yet it's trapped in my head and consequently turns against me, flattening me with a suicidal depression. If anyone thinks they have got any answers then write to me with them, because I'm completely lost here!